©1988 Autumn Publishing Ltd

Designed and produced by
Autumn Publishing Limited,
10 Eastgate Square, Chichester, England

Illustrated by Borivoj Likić
This 1988 edition published by Derrydale Books, imprint distributed
by Crown Publishers, Inc.,
225 Park Avenue South
New York
New York 10003

Typeset by Words&Spaces, Rowlands Castle, Hampshire
Printed in Czechoslovakia

ISBN 0 517 64979 9

hgfedcba

365
QUESTIONS
and ANSWERS

DERRYDALE BOOKS
New York

JANUARY

January 1 — HOW WAS THE EARTH FORMED?

There are several ideas, or theories, about the origin of the earth. One is that it was formed when a lump of glowing material became separated from the sun. The most popular theory, however, is that it was formed from a mass of gases and dust which were floating in space around the sun.

When this mass became the round ball we know as the earth, it continued to move around the sun. The earth is one of nine major planets, and many minor ones, which revolve around the sun. These planets and the sun form our solar system.

January 2 — WHY DO STARS SHINE?

In the universe there are many suns like the one which lights and heats up the earth and the other planets in our solar system. These suns are known as stars. Just like our sun, they produce their own light as they burn themselves up.

Their brightness reaches us in the form of small points of even light because they are so far away. Their distance from the earth is so great that we need a special unit to measure it. This is known as a light-year: that is, the distance that light travels during one year in space.

WHY DON'T STARS SHINE IN THE DAYTIME?

January 3

The layer of air that surrounds the earth is transparent. During the day it absorbs light from the sun and becomes a bluish color. This is why the sky is blue in the daytime. It is because this light is so bright and the light from the stars so weak that we cannot see the stars during the day. They do not show up until nighttime when the sky is dark, and if there are no clouds to hide them.

WHY DON'T WE SEE THE MOON ON SOME NIGHTS?

January 4

There are several reasons why we do not see the moon on some nights. The moon does not give out its own light but reflects light from the sun. Therefore, when the earth comes between the sun and the moon, it casts a shadow over the moon. This is known as an eclipse. When the moon moves between the earth and the sun only its far side is lit by the sun's rays. The side facing Earth is in total darkness. We call this a ''new'' moon. Finally, on nights when the sky is overcast, the clouds hide the moon from us.

WHY IS THE MOON NOT ALWAYS COMPLETELY ROUND?

January 5

The sun always lights up half of the moon's surface, the part facing the sun. But, as the moon moves around the earth and the earth moves around the sun, different parts of the sunlit moon are visible to us. Sometimes we see the whole of the sunlit surface; this is what we call the ''full'' moon. Sometimes we see only the left or right part, which looks like a slice of melon. So we see the moon in several stages. These are called phases of the moon and are known as: full moon, waning moon, new moon and waxing moon.

January
6

WHY DOES THE MOON SEEM TO MOVE WITH US?

If we look at the moon when we walk outdoors at night, it seems to be moving with us. In fact, the moon moves much faster than we do. But, because it is so far away, it appears to move at the same speed.

To appreciate its real change of position we would have to cover distances so great that we would need to travel in a spaceship. So the appearance of the moon moving with us is just an illusion.

January
7

HOW DOES DAY TURN INTO NIGHT?

As the earth moves around the sun, it also spins round on its axis. This means that different parts of the earth are lit up at different times. When our part of the earth is lit up, it is daytime for us. As we move around, away from the sun, it becomes dark and we can see the stars; this is nighttime.

The sun appears to move across the sky, but in fact the earth is moving around the sun.

January 8

WHY IS IT COLD IN SOME PLACES IN THE WORLD AND HOT IN OTHERS?

January 9

WHY IS THE TIME DIFFERENT IN OTHER COUNTRIES?

Where the sun's rays shine directly on the earth at right angles, they produce the maximum amount of heat. This happens at the equator, which is the hottest part of the earth.

Where the sun's rays fall at a slanting angle to the earth they provide less heat. Therefore, The North Pole and the South Pole are the coldest places. As you travel further from the equator the weather becomes cooler. In Africa, for example, it is much hotter than in northern Europe.

It is also colder at high altitudes, so a mountaintop is colder than a valley.

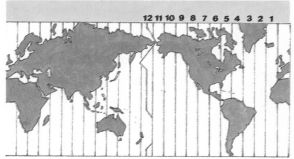

The time it takes for the earth to make one rotation has been divided into 24 parts known as hours. This division was made to give us a fixed unit of time.

We take as a reference point the moment when the sun is at its highest point in the sky (when the shade is at its minimum). This is called mid-day, or noon.

However, this does not happen at the same moment on each part of the earth because the earth is turning all the time. Therefore, when it is mid-day in London it will be seven o'clock in the morning in some parts of the United States of America. Because the U.S.A. is such a large country, there are even time differences between some of the states.

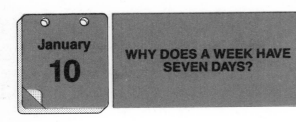

MONDAY

TUESDAY

WEDNESDAY

THURSDAY

FRIDAY

SATURDAY

SUNDAY

The Bible says that God created the universe in six days and that the seventh was a day of rest. It was the ancient Jews who adopted the seven-day week and made one of them (the Sabbath) a religious festival. The Romans dedicated Sunday to the sun, Monday to the moon, Tuesday to Mars, Wednesday to Mercury, Thursday to Jupiter, Friday to Venus, and Saturday to Saturn. The Christians later dedicated Sunday to the Lord (Domenicus).

In the English calendar, Monday came from the Old English for Moon Day; Tuesday, Wednesday, and Thursday were derived from the names of Germanic gods similar to the Roman ones. Friday is derived from a Norse and Teutonic goddess-Frigg or Frigga. Saturday comes from the Latin for Saturn.

A year is the time it takes for the earth to travel once around the sun. This period was divided into units of months and there are twelve in one year.

Our calendar comes from that worked out by a Greek astronomer employed by Julius Caesar. A modification was later made by Pope Gregory XIII and the calendar used now is known as the Gregorian calendar.

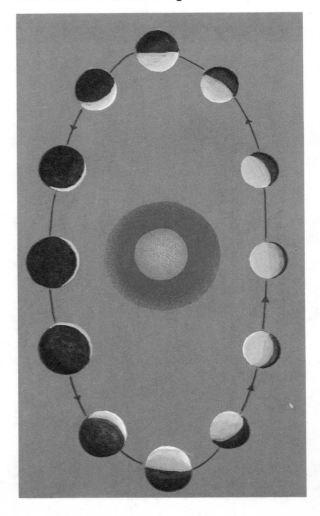

January 12 — WHY IS THE SKY BLUE DURING THE DAY?

White light is made up of different colors, one of which is blue. The ozone in the atmosphere absorbs some of the light from the sun and it takes on the blue color.
If you look at the sky from an airplane you will see that there is a darker band of blue where the ozone layer is concentrated. The ozone layer protects the earth by absorbing harmful rays from the sun.

January 13 — HOW ARE MOUNTAINS FORMED?

Earth's crust has many elevated features which we call mountains. The mountains we know today are the result of millions of years of geological activity. They have formed in several ways: from fractures in the surface of the earth; from volcanic eruptions; from materials which have built up over the years on the ocean beds and have later been pushed upward. They are also formed by the earth being worn away in places and creating large mounds.

January 14 — HOW DO VOLCANOES FORM?

The interior of the earth is made of molten rock. Pressures build up in this melted mass (magma) and force the earth's crust to crack open. Large quantities of hot material called lava escape through the crack, along with steam, gases, ash, and rock.

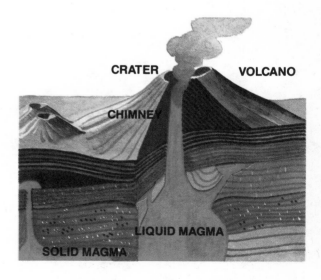

CRATER   VOLCANO
CHIMNEY
LIQUID MAGMA
SOLID MAGMA

As the lava pours out, it cools and becomes solid. This material builds up around the opening (crater) and forms the side of the volcano.

January 15 — WHY DO EARTHQUAKES OCCUR?

Earthquakes and tremors in the earth are caused by movements in the earth's interior. The vibration from the earthquake makes the surface of the earth shake. If the quake or tremor is strong it may cause cracks in the ground. In built-up areas buildings may be damaged. Scientists who study earthquakes are using their knowledge to predict when they might happen so that damage and loss of life can be avoided.

January 16 — WHAT CAUSES ECHOES?

Sound is transmitted by means of waves. If these waves meet an obstacle they collide with it and bounce back. So we hear not only the original sound but also the repetition of the sound as it bounces back to us. This is called an echo.

If we tried to produce an echo in a room, we would not be able to hear it. This is because the distance is so short and the spread of sound so rapid that the original sound and the echo are heard at the same time. However, if you shout very loudly in the mountains, you will hear both sounds so clearly that you may think someone is calling back to you.

January 17 — WHY ARE SOME RIVERBEDS DRY IN SUMMER?

The water of a river comes from rain water and melted snow from mountains. We call this the source of the river.

In winter, snow and rain provide water to the rivers. During the summer, however, there is less rain and no snow, so there is less water in the rivers. The heat of the sun also causes some of the water to evaporate. In a very hot, dry summer some riverbeds may become completely dry.

When we have a very hot summer with very little rain, and the lakes and rivers dry up, it is called a drought.

the water wears away the ground and the natural path of the river is formed. As the river reaches flatter ground, it slows down. Eventually it flows into a lake or the sea.

WHY ARE STONES IN A RIVER SMOOTH?

January 19

The current of a river drags along large quantities of stones. You may have noticed how round and smooth they are. Their rough edges have been worn away as the stones have been knocked against each other and been rubbed against the river bed. The surface of the stones has also been smoothed by the movement of the water over the years. When these stones are quite large they are known as boulders.

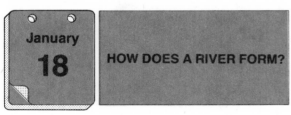

HOW DOES A RIVER FORM?

January 18

Rain water and melted snow collect in hollows in high ground such as mountains and hills. The water then flows downward by the steepest route. The steeper the slope, the faster the river flows. As time passes,

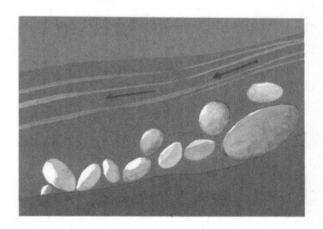

January 20

WHY DOES IT RAIN?

The heat of the sun causes the surface of the sea to evaporate. The vapor that forms rises because it is lighter than air. This concentrated vapor is a mass of minute particles of water which forms clouds that are blown inland by the wind. If the temperature goes down or the mass of clouds crosses a cold zone in the atmosphere, the drops of water get larger. When these drops become heavier than air they fall as rain.

January 21

WHY DOES THUNDER ALWAYS FOLLOW LIGHTNING?

Storms are caused by an electrical disturbance in the atmosphere. The electrical pressure between two clouds or between a cloud and the ground gives off sparks of electricity called lightning, and causes a rumbling sound known as thunder. Thunder and lightning occur at the same time, but we see the lightning before we hear the thunder because light travels faster than sound. That is why thunder always follows lightning.

January 22

WHY DO RAINBOWS OCCUR?

A rainbow appears in the sky when there is rain while the sun is shining. As the sunlight passes through the raindrops at an angle, the light is reflected. This causes the light to break up into the seven colors that make up white light. These colors form an arch, which we see as a rainbow.

The colors of a rainbow are red, orange, yellow, green, blue, indigo, and violet.

January
23

WHAT CAUSES FOG?

When water on the surface of the sea or rivers turns into vapor, the vapor rises because it weighs less than the air. It then condenses in the air as cloud. But if the temperature is very low or the air is humid, this condensation takes place near the ground. This results in fog or mist which is like a cloud at ground level. It usually occurs in the evening or early morning when the sun does not give much heat.

When fog forms over the sea, foghorns are used to warn ships.

January
24

WHY CAN WE FEEL THE AIR BUT NOT SEE IT?

The air is made up of various elements of which the most important are oxygen and nitrogen. The tiny molecules of air are separate from each other and allow light to pass through. This is why we cannot see the air. But we can feel it on our skin, especially when the air is very hot or very cold. We can also feel it when it moves.

The air moves when the layers near the earth become warm. This warm air is lighter so it rises. As this air rises it forces the colder air to move down and occupy the empty space. So there is a continuous movement of air, upward and downward.

January
25

HOW DO CLOUDS MOVE IN THE SKY?

We now know that clouds form from water vapor which comes from the evaporation of seas and rivers. The water vapor condenses into many tiny droplets of water. These small drops fall very slowly so it seems as if they are floating in the sky.

When the wind blows it pulls the clouds with it and makes them travel at the same speed, so it looks as if the clouds are

During the night, as the temperature drops, this vapor turns into liquid on any solid surface. So it forms tiny drops of water on the earth, rocks, grass, and plants. This is known as dew. If you go out into the garden early in the morning you will find the grass quite wet.

In winter, when it is very cold, this vapor turns first into a liquid, then it freezes. So it forms tiny ice crystals, which we call frost. On a cold morning you will see frost lying on the ground, on fences, plants, and cars.

January 27

WHY DOES IT SNOW IN WINTER?

moving by themselves. If you go up a mountain you may find yourself in the middle of a cloud.

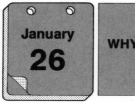

January 26

WHY DO FROST AND DEW FORM?

As the earth spins round, it is also tilted on its axis. When the tilt is away from the sun, the earth receives less of the sun's heat. This is the winter season when the weather is cold.

The air surrounding the earth also contains a certain amount of water vapor. This is known as the atmospheric humidity.

When it is very cold the drops of water which make up clouds freeze and form tiny crystals. These crystals form clusters which make up snowflakes and they fall to the ground without melting. They pile up and form quite a solid mass. If you catch a snowflake and put it under a microscope, you will see that it forms a very pretty pattern. The wonderful thing is that each snowflake has a different pattern.

WHY DO WE SOMETIMES SEE A REFLECTION IN WATER?

January 28

When light shines on a pool of water it is dispersed in three ways.

Some of it is absorbed as heat. Some of it passes through the water and is deflected or "bent." This phenomenon is known as refraction of light.

Finally, some of the light is reflected on the surface of the water. So the water is like a mirror. If the pool of water is very clean and clear it is possible to see a reflection very clearly.

WHY DOES THE SEA HAVE WAVES?

January 29

When the wind blows on the sea it moves the water and causes a swell. So waves rise up on the surface of the sea. The size and speed of the waves depends on the strength of the wind.

Giant waves, which can reach up to 20 meters/65 feet in height, have a different origin. They are caused by movements in the interior of the earth, below the ocean bed. They are known as tidal waves and can cause much damage. They occur mainly in the Pacific Ocean, but are rare.

WHY IS SEA WATER SALTY?

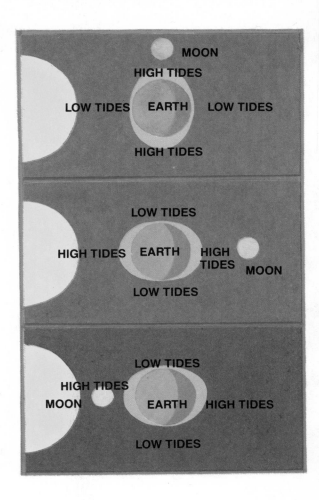

As rivers flow toward the sea, the water takes with it salts and other materials from the surface of rocks. These dissolve and are deposited in the sea. The evaporation of the water by the sun keeps the water level the same, but it causes concentration in the accumulation of salts. This makes the sea water taste very salty.

The level of concentration of salts is known as the salinity. Some oceans are more salty than others.

The most common salt substance is sodium chloride, or common salt. This is the salt we use on our food. It is taken from the sea by evaporation. The sea water is cut off in shallow land. When it has evaporated, crystallized salt is left behind and this is collected for our use.

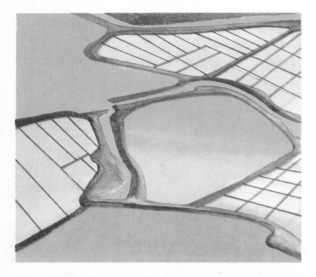

January
31

WHY DOES THE SEA GO IN AND OUT?

If you have visited the seaside you may have noticed that the sea moves in and out. Sometimes it is high up on the beach, sometimes it is a long way out. These

movements of the sea are called tides. When the sea is high up it is high tide, when it is a long way out, it is low tide.

The tides are caused by the movements of the moon around the earth and the earth around the sun. Both the sun and the moon have an influence on the earth, called gravity – this is a force of attraction. This pull from the sun and moon causes a slight bulge in the earth's surface. As the earth turns round, this pull causes movements of the oceans called tides. A high tide occurs about every twelve hours.

The parts of the earth nearest and furthest from the sun and moon are most affected by this gravitational pull. But because the moon is nearer it has a greater influence. When the moon is new or full (and the sun, moon and earth are in a straight line), the pull is strongest. This is when we have the highest tides, called spring tides. At half moon the tides are at their lowest. These are called neap tides.

FEBRUARY

February 1

WHAT ARE METEORS AND METEORITES?

On a clear night you may notice a trail of many particles of light flash across the sky. These shooting stars are called meteors. They are made up of solid particles from space. As they move very fast they get very hot, so they usually melt before they reach the earth. Because they are so hot they give out light. It is this flashing light we see as they move across the sky.

Meteorites are larger pieces of rock from space. Because they are larger than meteors, they do not burn up completely when they enter the earth's atmosphere, and they fall to the ground.

Meteorites vary in weight. In Devil's Canyon, Arizona, a meteorite made a crater of 1,265 meters (4150 feet) across and 175 meters (575 feet) deep.

February 2

WHY DON'T PLANTS GROW IN THE DESERT?

Plants and trees need water in order to grow. Deserts are areas of the earth which are so dry that plants cannot grow there. The dryness is mainly caused by lack of rain. In deserts where there is rain, the heat is so intense that the water evaporates very quickly. Hot winds also dry up the rain water. In some places the rain falls into cracks in rocks and goes beyond the reach of the roots of plants.

The surface of a desert is usually sand or rock. There are often such strong winds that the sand is blown into piles called sand dunes. Deserts are found in parts of the tropics and in the interiors of large continents such as Australia.

February 3

WHY DO COMETS HAVE TAILS?

Comets travel around the sun. They are made of ice, gas, and dust left over from the formation of the solar system.

As a comet moves near the sun, some of the gases burn up and shoot out its nucleus to form a tail. The speed of the

The surface water of the sea is constantly being turned into vapor by the heat of the sun. This evaporation keeps the level of the sea the same.

There is one event which could increase the volume of the sea. If the temperature around the two poles increased, this could melt the polar ice caps. Then the water level of the oceans would rise and this could cause serious flooding of some parts of the earth.

comet increases as it nears the sun. At its nearest point to the sun, it reaches its maximum size and brightness. As it moves away from the sun, particles from the comet's head are blown by the solar wind. These particles form the tail of the comet. So when the comet moves away from the sun, it goes tail first.

February 5 — WHAT ARE THE NORTHERN LIGHTS?

February 4 — WHY DOESN'T THE SEA FLOOD THE EARTH?

Sometimes brilliant displays of colored lights can be seen in the northern skies. These are called the Northern Lights. They are caused by flares from the sun. These flares send out millions of tiny particles which travel to the earth. As they collide with the atoms and molecules in the earth's atmosphere, they send out light. These lights can best be seen from northern Scotland, northern Norway and Sweden, and the Hudson Bay area of Canada. There are similar lights over the South Pole.

<table>
<tr><td> **February 6**</td><td>**WHY DO SOME RIVERS HAVE A DELTA?**</td></tr>
</table>

Greeks who sailed to Egypt noticed that the forked mouth of the River Nile formed, with the sea, a triangular piece of land. They called it a delta after the fourth letter of the Greek alphabet, which is the shape of a triangle.

A delta is formed when a muddy river flows very slowly into the sea. Because the water is flowing slowly, the mud does not get washed out to sea. It builds up around the mouth of the river.

The largest delta is formed by the Mississippi River in the USA.

<table>
<tr><td>**February 7**</td><td>**WHAT IS SAINT ELMO'S FIRE?**</td></tr>
</table>

A discharge of atmospheric electricity can appear as a tip of light on the mast of a ship. But in former times sailors had no explanation for this. So the story came about that it was a sign from Saint Elmo, the patron saint of sailors, that he was watching over them. Saint Elmo, an Italian, was an early Christian bishop and was adopted by sailors from the Mediteranean countries as their saint.

<table>
<tr><td> **February 8**</td><td>**WHAT IS A CYCLONE?**</td></tr>
</table>

A cyclone is a very strong wind that rotates in a spiral. It is caused by a drop in atmospheric pressure. In the southern hemisphere the wind goes in a clock-wise spiral; in the northern hemisphere it is anti-clockwise.

Tropical cyclones are known as hurricanes in the Atlantic and Caribbean; typhoons in the West Pacific and China Sea.

These winds can cause a lot of damage to life and property. When they come from the sea they can cause flooding.

February 9

WHY IS THERE WIND?

Wind is movement of the air and is caused by different pressures in the atmosphere. Air moves from high-pressure areas to low-pressure areas. Also, warm air from the ground moves up and cold air takes its place. Sea breezes occur because warm air from the land rises and cooler air from the sea moves to the land. At night, however, because the land cools more quickly than the sea, warm air rises from the sea and cooler air from the land blows onto the sea. The wind is measured by wind gauges and weather vanes.

February 10

WHY DO WE ALWAYS SEE THE SAME SIDE OF THE MOON?

The Moon, like the Earth, has two movements. It moves around the Earth, just as the Earth moves around the Sun. And it also spins round on its own axis. The time it takes to spin is the same as the time it takes to move once around the Earth.

So the same part of the Moon always faces the Earth. As we hadn't been able to observe the far side of the Moon with a telescope, we knew very little about it until spacemen landed there and were able to explore the other side.

February 11

WHY DOES A DRY ROAD SOMETIMES LOOK WET?

You may have noticed, when travelling by car on a hot, sunny day, that the road seems wet and gives a reflection. This is known as a 'mirror' effect. It happens when light passes through atmospheric layers of different intensity. The layer of air immediately above the tar produces an image which resembles the reflection on water. This phenomenon is quite common in the desert, where the heat and dryness create this shimmering effect.

February 12

HOW ARE WATERFALLS FORMED?

February 13

WHY DO ASTRONAUTS FLOAT IN SPACE?

Rivers have to make their way across the countryside from the hills and mountains where they start, always moving downhill towards the sea. Usually they wind through low-lying valleys. When they reach steep slopes or cliffs the water pours over the edge creating a waterfall. While it is still a stream, the waterfall is small. If a full river falls over a large cliff the effect is spectacular. There are large and beautiful waterfalls in various parts of the world: one of the most famous is the Niagara Falls on the borders between Canada and the U.S.A. The power of the water is so great that in 300 years it has worn away 500 meters (1,600 feet) of rock.

Every object exerts a force of attraction on other objects. This is called the force of gravity. Because the earth's gravity is very strong it pulls things toward it like a

magnet. If you drop an object, it doesn't just fall to the ground, it is pulled to the ground by this force. This is what gives everything weight and keeps it on Earth.

As we travel away from the earth, the earth's gravity has less influence. This is why astronauts float inside a spaceship. They are so far from the earth that the earth's gravity has little effect. So they become "weightless."

February 14

WHAT CAUSES STRANGE ROCK FORMATIONS?

Over the years, wind, rain, sea, and rivers can wear away rock into strange and interesting shapes. Sometimes rocks have the shapes of buildings. For example, there is a maze of rocks in Spain which looks like a city. They are called the Enchanted City of Cuenca. In Arizona, there is a place called Monument Valley, where the rocks look like monuments. It took two million years for the Colorado River to cut away the Grand Canyon in the United States.

February 15

HOW DO ICEBERGS FORM?

Icebergs come from glaciers – a glacier is a sheet of ice which forms on the mountainside and in polar regions. When the ice of a glacier reaches the sea, bits of it break off and form icebergs. They can float quite a long way in the ocean. Usually only the tip of the iceberg shows above the water, so icebergs can be a danger to ships. In 1912 the *Titanic*, a large passenger liner on her first voyage from England to New York collided with an iceberg and sank.

February 16

HOW IS COAL MADE?

Coal is formed from the remains of trees and plants which grew millions of years ago. They decayed and sank into the ground, and were pressed under layers of rock and other minerals.

As this vegetation dried up, it turned into peat, then into coal. The coal is found underground in layers called seams. Mines have to be made in order to dig it out. Coal is a very useful product. Not only is it used as fuel but also in the manufacture of such things as dyes and insecticides.

COAL

FOREST

DECAYING FOREST

SEA OVER DECAY

ROCKS FORMING

COAL SEAM

because the interior of the earth is hot. Rain water that has gone down cracks deep into the earth becomes heated. The hot water is then forced up out of the ground under pressure.

Some hot springs come from volcanic rock nearer the surface. These are called geysers. Hot water and steam is forced out of a tubular crack in the ground and spurts quite high in the air. There is a geyser in Yellowstone National Park called Old Faithful because it erupts every 65 minutes without fail. It reaches a height of about 50 meters (164 feet).

February
17

WHY DOES HOT WATER COME OUT OF THE GROUND?

February
18

WHY DO WE LOVE THE SUN?

Water gushing from a crack in the ground is called a spring. If the water comes from deep down in the ground it is hot. This is

The sun is essential for life on Earth. Without it we would have no heat, light, or plants. If the sun were extinguished the

RA

HELIUS

earth would soon become a frozen, lifeless ball.

The warmth and light of the sun also make life much more pleasant. Perhaps it is for this reason that it has been worshipped as a god by many civilizations. To the ancient Egyptians it was known as the god Ra, and to the Greeks it was the god Helius.

We know that on a warm, sunny day most people feel more cheerful than on a cloudy and damp day.

February 19

WHY DO WE NEED WIND?

Although very strong winds can cause damage, the movement of air is very important to us. This is because the wind moves the clouds which bring rain. Without rain, plants would die and human beings and animals would have no food and water. Wind also carries warm air to colder areas that need its heat. Another important function of the wind today is to prevent polluted air from becoming concentrated in the atmosphere.

In the past sailors needed wind to sail their ships because there were no motor vessels then. Wind was also needed to turn windmills, which were used to pump water and to grind corn. Windmills can still be seen in some countries.

February 20

WHAT IS THE MIDNIGHT SUN?

Because the earth tilts slightly as it rotates, there is a time in the year, called the summer solstice, when one of the poles is tilted towards the sun. At this time the sun is visible in that area for 24 hours of the day and it is possible to see the sun at midnight.

WHY DOES SMOKE COME FROM MANURE HEAPS?

Manure heaps are made up of used hay and straw and some animal dung. When these materials have rotted they make a valuable fertilizer for plants. While the material is rotting, much chemical activity is taking place encouraged by the warm, damp conditions. As heat builds up in the heap, gases are formed which give off steam. That is why a manure heap seems to have smoke coming from it.

When the manure is ready it is spread over the ground.

HOW ARE UNDERGROUND CAVES FORMED?

Caves form in areas where there is limestone rock. As rivers or rain water flow over limestone some of the water trickles down deep holes in the rock and flows below the ground. The water gradually dissolves the limestone, creating caves and tunnels underground.

These caves often have icicle shapes hanging from the roof. They are called stalactites. They form as water slowly drips from the roof, leaving behind some of the limestone dissolved in it. As the drips reach the ground, "fingers" of limestone grow up from the ground. These formations are called stalagmites.

You can visit underground caves in many countries.

February 23 — WHY ARE OCEAN CURRENTS IMPORTANT?

The water in the ocean is always moving. Slow-moving water is called a drift. Rapidly moving water is called an ocean current. Currents are caused partly by the winds and partly by the movement of the earth as it rotates. Changes in temperature also cause water to move. This is because cold water, which is heavier, pushes warm water out of the way. Currents of warm water can

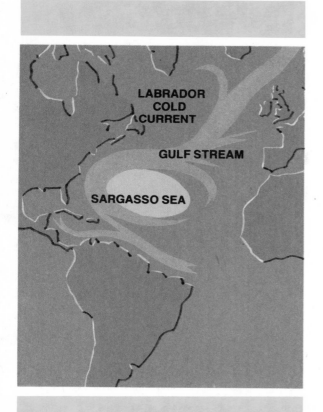

LABRADOR COLD CURRENT

GULF STREAM

SARGASSO SEA

affect the climate. For example, the Gulf Stream carries warm air to Western Europe and makes winters less severe. The cold Labrador Current (of northern origin) produces colder winters on the eastern coast of North America. The main oceans of the world are the Pacific, the Atlantic, the Indian, and the Arctic.

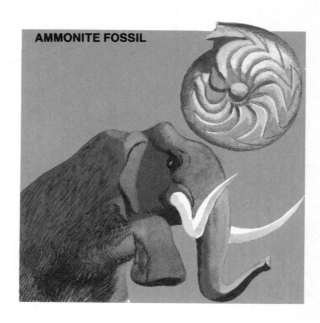

AMMONITE FOSSIL

February 24 — WHAT ARE FOSSILS?

Fossils are the remains or traces of animals, insects, and plants which have been trapped in rocks. Their imprint is left in the rock. Even an animal's footprints can become fossilized. Sometimes a whole animal can be preserved intact. Animal remains have been found preserved in Siberian glaciers and Polish mines. Many insects have been preserved in the amber (hardened resin) of ancient pine trees.

By studying fossils, scientists can work out how plants and animals have evolved over the years.

Fossils also help in discovering the age of rocks. When you are on vacation in the country or near the sea, you may like to look for fossils in rocks.

February 25 — WHY DO RIVERS MEANDER?

A meander is a curve in a river. When a river reaches flat ground it flows very

slowly. Because there is very little current, the water is forced to go around obstacles or to follow slopes in the ground. The banks become curved as the current is pushed from right to left and left to right. The force of the current hollows out one bank and deposits mud on the opposite bank. Some meanders form oxbow lakes (shaped in a loop). If the river dries up temporarily these lakes become cut off.

We use the word "meander" to describe the way someone walks. That is, when a person is wandering aimlessly, we say he is meandering.

February
26

HOW DO GLACIERS FORM?

Glaciers are great sheets of ice formed from years of unmelted snow which has been compacted and turned into ice. Some glaciers form down the sides of mountains and are known as valley glaciers. Others form in polar regions and are known as sheet glaciers. Because they are in very cold regions they do not melt. This is fortunate because they make up 10 per cent of the surface of the earth, and if they did melt they would cause the ocean level to rise.

February
27

HOW ARE ATOLLS FORMED?

An atoll is a circular coral island surrounding a shallow lagoon. It is made up of corals — tiny sea animals which live in warm waters. During the latter part of their life they remain fastened to rocks on the bottom of the sea. When the coral dies the

skeleton remains and other corals grow on top of them. Over the years, a coral island is made.

Another type of coral island is called a reef. The most famous is the Great Barrier Reef in Australia which is many miles in length.

These reefs are very beautiful and are a popular tourist attraction. The coral is collected and made into jewelry.

February
28

HOW ARE SEASIDE CAVES FORMED?

SOFT ROCK

Caves are formed when the water runs over soft rock for a long time. Along the coast, the sea is constantly washing against the rocks. The bigger the waves, the more rock is eroded (worn away). If part of the rock is softer than the rest, the sea cuts through it more quickly and forms a cave. The rocky pillars and arches you can see off some coast lines are the remains of caves where the sea has eroded most of the rock, leaving only the very hardest part.

MARCH

A baby is made by the father's sperm joining with the mother's egg and fertilizing it. This is called conception. The baby grows inside the mother in a kind of bag called the womb. As the baby grows and gets bigger, the mother's stomach swells. This is why the mother gains weight when she is expecting a baby (that is, when she is pregnant).

It takes about three months for the baby to become completely formed. In this time the mother does not get much bigger. But, as the baby grows to his full size, the mother's body expands. Most babies weigh at least 3 kilograms (6½ lbs) when they are born. After the birth, the mother regains her normal size and shape.

March
2

WHY DOES A WOMAN GO TO THE HOSPITAL TO HAVE A BABY?

Not very long ago most mothers used to give birth at home. They were helped by a nurse called a midwife. Now they usually go to a hospital in case they need the help of a doctor or need medicine.

The baby is ready to be born about nine months after conception. The mother knows the baby is ready to come into the world because she feels some pain or pressure in her womb. That is when she goes to the hospital.

Giving birth is a natural occurrence. It consists of the tightening and slackening of the walls of the mother's womb. These movements help the mother to push the baby out of the womb.

The process can be slow and painful. However, the staff at the hospital make sure that both mother and baby are safe and comfortable. So if your mother has to go to the hospital to give you a baby brother or sister, you will know that she will be taken care of and given all the attention she needs.

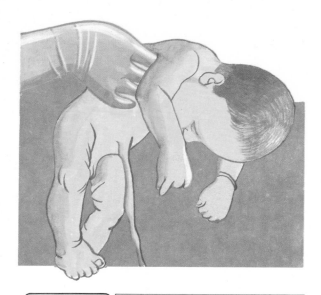

and they have to crawl on all fours first. Man also has a longer life than most animals and he takes longer to grow into an adult. Therefore, the baby stage lasts longer.

Also, offspring of animals often have to start looking after themselves when they are very young, so they need to be able to walk as early as possible.

The baby grows in the womb for nine months. This is called the gestation period. It is quiet and dark there, and he feels warm and comfortable. So, when he is born, the light and sudden movement of his new surroundings may frighten him, and make him feel unsafe. He usually screws up his face and cries, which makes him look wrinkled and not very pretty. The skin on his body looks wrinkled too because it hasn't yet absorbed enough moisture. However, he soon fills out and his skin becomes smooth.

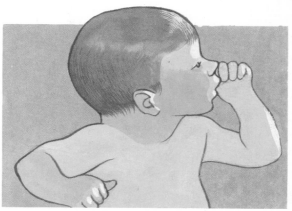

From the moment of birth a baby can carry out all natural functions, just like any animal's offspring. However, unlike other species, a human baby cannot walk right away. This is partly because man walks on two legs whereas animals walk on four legs. It is more difficult for babies to learn to walk

When a baby leaves the mother's womb to live in the outside world his small stomach does not immediately adapt to solid food. This is why the baby needs milk. Teeth are not needed for this type of food because the baby does not have to chew. Indeed, they would be in the way

since the baby has to suck his food into his mouth. And it would not be very comfortable for the mother to breast-feed a baby who had a mouthful of teeth.

As the baby grows, teeth begin to appear in the gums of his mouth. This stage is called teething. It can be a little painful for the baby and he may cry when his teeth come through. When the baby has teeth he can start to eat solid foods.

It is very important to look after a child's teeth right from the start. This is one reason why babies need milk because the calcium in it helps to make teeth grow healthy and strong.

March 6

WHY DO WE HAVE A NAVEL?

When a baby is in the mother's womb he is not fed through the mouth. Food reaches the baby through a tube which comes from a bag called the placenta. The tube is attached to the baby's stomach. This tube is known as the umbilical cord.

After the baby is born he can be fed through the mouth, so the placenta is no longer needed. The doctor cuts the cord, leaving a scar in the center of the baby's belly. This scar, which remains throughout life, is called the navel. You probably call this little mark your belly button.

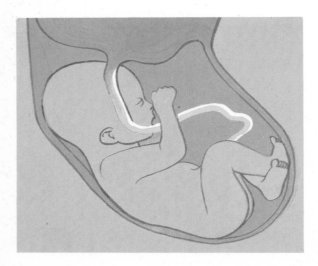

March 7

WHY DON'T BABIES HAVE TAILS LIKE MONKEYS?

It has been proved that the main use of an animal's tail is to maintain balance. In the case of monkeys, who have long tails, it helps them move from tree to tree. This is very useful for them because they live in trees and find food there.

In primitive times, man may have lived in trees. According to some experts he had a tail which he used in the same way as monkeys use theirs. When man adapted to walking upright and living on the ground, he no longer needed a tail. Therefore, as man progressed and developed, the tail disappeared. This explains why, today, man has only the remains of a tail – that is, the small bone called the coccyx at the base of the spine.

March 8

WHY ARE SOME BABIES BREAST-FED AND SOME BOTTLE-FED?

The ideal food for a baby is mother's milk which is stored in her breasts. Breast-feeding also makes a loving link between mother and child. If the mother is not well enough to breast-feed her baby, or does not have enough milk, she may decide to feed the baby from a bottle. This bottled milk contains everything the baby needs. By cuddling the baby when feeding him from a bottle, the mother can give the baby the same loving feeling he gets when on the breast. A mother may also use the bottle sometimes for convenience: for example, when she is traveling or in public places.

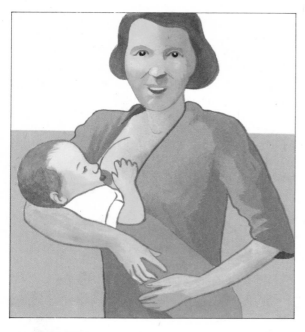

March
9

WHY DO WE GROW WITHOUT REALLY NOTICING?

When a human being is born, he or she is completely formed. However, to reach the size of an adult, the body must gradually grow. The head needs to grow least, which is why children's heads look big for their bodies.

During growth, the cells of the body increase and then split up. This is a natural process, but is so slow that you do not realise it's happening. You'll notice you've got bigger when you find that you've grown out of some of your clothes. The body stops growing at about 20 years of age.

In order to grow and be healthy, we need energy-giving, nutritious food. So it is very important for growing people to have a healthy diet.

March
10

WHY DO WE FEEL HUNGRY AND THIRSTY?

Humans need food in order to grow and remain healthy. We also need food for energy. The human body is like a machine. It converts one form of energy into another. So the energy in food is converted by the body into other forms of energy; heat, movement and mental activity. When we need food or drink this sets off a kind of alarm system in the body. The empty stomach sends a message (via the nervous system) to the brain to make us think about

food and drink. We then feel hungry or thirsty and eat or drink to satisfy our needs. When the stomach is empty again we receive another signal that we need some food.

March 11

WHY DO WE FEEL SLEEPY?

During the day we use up a lot of energy which makes us tired at the end of the day. That is why we need to sleep at night. While we are sleeping, the activity of every part of the body slows down and the whole body gets a deep rest. In fact, not only the body becomes rested, but also the mind. A good night's sleep gives us back energy so that we can work and play the next day.

Small children also need a rest during the day as they cannot store as much energy as adults. When we feel sleepy it means we need a rest.

March 12

WHY DO WE SHUT OUR EYES WHEN WE GO TO SLEEP?

When you are awake the muscles of the eyelids are tightened, although you do not notice this. When you feel sleepy all the muscles begin to relax, your eyelids begin to droop and it is difficult to keep your eyes open. At the same time, all your other muscles relax. You may also notice that your arms and legs feel limp and your hands fall open. These feelings of relaxation are signs that you are tired and ready to fall asleep. When you are very tired you probably won't be able to keep your eyes open.

March 13

WHY DO SOME PEOPLE SNORE?

Snoring is the sound air makes when it passes over certain parts of the mouth and throat. It is a vibration which usually happens when a person sleeps lying on his back with his mouth open. The snoring may stop if he turns on his side. People who have catarrh often snore, because their throat and nasal cavities become coated with mucus. Smoking tobacco and drinking alcohol may also increase the amount of

mucus in the breathing system. So people who drink and smoke may snore. It is unusual for children to snore, but it can happen if the child has a bad cold.

March
14

WHY DO WE DREAM
WHEN WE ARE ASLEEP?

When we sleep, the heart continues to work. Dreams are a sign that there is still some activity going on in the brain. The part of the mind that is used in dreaming is called the unconscious mind. This means there is activity in the mind which we cannot control.

During a dream we may see pictures like a film or television. Sometimes we feel we are taking part in an event. Things we have done during the day often appear in our dreams in a very mixed-up way. Dreaming is a natural and healthy part of sleep.

March
15

HOW DO WE SPEAK?

Sounds are made by air passing through the larynx, or voice box, in the throat. The sound comes out through the mouth. You can make different sounds by pushing your mouth into different shapes. If you say all the vowel sounds, (a,e,i,o,u), in front of a mirror you will see that your mouth makes a different shape each time. If you want to say something loudly you need to pass more air through the mouth. This means you will need to take a deep breath before shouting or singing. If you want to whisper you do not need much air in the throat nor do you need to move the mouth as much.

March 16 — WHY DO WE CRY WHEN WE ARE SAD OR IN PAIN?

When we are in pain, or have received sad news, or are frightened or nervous, this affects our feelings, or emotions. Therefore, a message is sent to a certain part of the brain that we are sad or in pain. This sets off the release of tears through tubes called tear ducts. The tears are partly an alarm system. If you are in pain, you cry and get help. The tears also give a relief from tension. You will probably have noticed that after you have cried you feel relieved and sometimes happier.

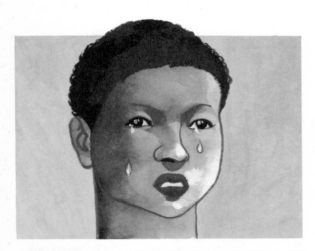

March 17 — WHY DO WE FEEL WARM WHEN WE RUN OR EXERCISE?

The human body is like a machine which transforms energy. The body changes energy from food into other kinds of energy. One form is called dynamic energy. This is developed in the muscles. When the muscles are used in exercise or running, part of the energy is turned into heat—thermal energy. If you run very fast more heat is produced. This is why you feel warm when you have been playing games or running races.

You may have noticed that when you get very hot during exercise you sweat, or perspire. This is the body's way of reducing its own heat. The water that comes out of the pores of the skin (perspiration) cools the body so that it does not become overheated.

March 18 — WHY DO WE SHIVER WHEN WE ARE COLD?

The body's normal temperature is 36 degrees centigrade. If, for any reason, this temperature changes, the body naturally adjusts. Just as the body cools itself by sweating when it becomes hot, it reacts in a similar way when it becomes cold. When we become very cold, we either move about to get warm or shiver. Shivering is a natural movement the body makes to get warm. So, if we don't deliberately move, the body will make some movement independent of our will. This is called involuntary movement.

When we shiver thousands of little muscular fibers move. Also, goose pimples appear on the skin and little hairs stand on end. This helps to increase the circulation of air on the skin and warm it up.

March
20

WHY DOES SMOKE SEEM TO COME OUT OF MOUTHS IN COLD WEATHER?

When we breathe out, air comes out of our mouths. Because the air has been in the body it is very warm. When the air temperature outside is warm we do not notice breath as it comes out. However, when the outside air is very cold, warm breath condenses in the cold air. The water vapor in our breath forms tiny droplets of water, similar to the way clouds form. This is why we can see breath, which looks like smoke in the cold air.

You may have noticed this effect in animals. If you have watched a horse running around in cold weather you will have seen that he has great clouds of "smoke" coming from his nostrils.

March
19

WHY DOESN'T IT HURT WHEN WE HAVE OUR HAIR CUT?

The root of the hair is situated in the second layer of skin. In this area there are nerve endings. This means that if someone pulls out one of our hairs, we feel some pain. The actual hair itself, however, does not have nerves. So when someone cuts our hair we do not feel anything. Of course, if the person tugged our hair at the same time we would feel that because he would be pulling at the roots. But cutting is painless, so don't be afraid to get a haircut.

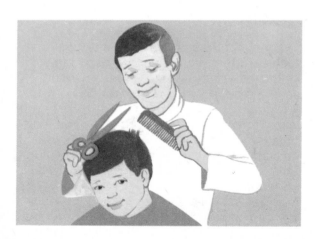

WHY DO SOME MEN GO BALD?

Baldness is absence of hair on the scalp. It affects men more than women because male hormones play a part in the process of balding. Over a period of time, greasy substances build up in the tiny blood vessels that feed the root of the hair. This slows down, or stops, the flow of blood to the root which weakens the hair and causes it to fall out. Some men whose bodies produce a lot of the greasy substances begin to lose their hair when they are quite young.

Illness or a very bad shock or emotional experience can cause hair to go gray. In some families, people tend to go gray early, just as in some families men tend to go bald early in life.

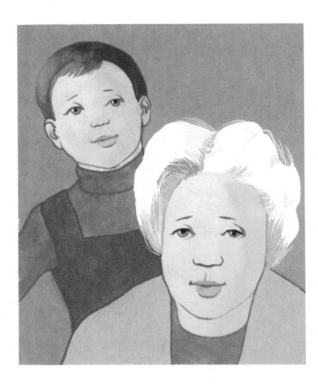

WHY DO OLD PEOPLE HAVE GREY HAIR?

The color of the hair is produced by a substance called melanin. This is the same substance that produces the color of skin and protects it from the sun. As time passes and a person becomes older, less melanin is produced. Therefore, the hair begins to lose its color and becomes gray. This can happen even before old age.

WHY DO OLD PEOPLE HAVE WRINKLES?

The smoothness of a child's skin is due to the amount of water contained in the cells of the body. As time passes, those cells are not able to hold so much water. The body does not replace all the water that is lost through perspiration, for example. This lack of moisture means the skin loses its elasticity and makes the skin shrivel up. This is why old people have wrinkles.

People who live in very hot, dry countries may get wrinkles sooner than people who live in a cooler, damper climate. There are

several kinds of creams and lotions which can be put on skin to help keep its moisture and smoothness.

March 24

WHY DO SOME PEOPLE HAVE FRECKLES?

The color of skin is due to a substance called melanin. This substance helps to protect skin from harmful rays of the sun. These rays can cause skin to burn. People who live in hot countries have darker skin to protect them from the sun.

Freckles, tiny brown spots on the face and arms, are also caused by melanin. These small brown spots are due to uneven distribution of melanin in the skin. They are more noticeable when a person has been in the sunlight. People with a fair complexion and fair or red hair tend to have freckles. We should all take care not to stay in the hot sun too long, but fair people need to be more careful.

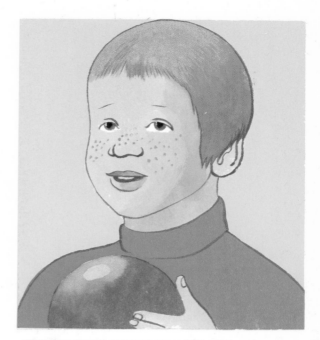

March 25

WHY DO HEIGHTS MAKE SOME PEOPLE FEEL DIZZY?

45

When some people are in a high place, and not used to heights, they may be afraid of falling. This fear affects the nervous system and confused messages are sent to the brain. While they know they are in a safe place, they also feel as though they are falling. This makes them feel dizzy and a little sick — an unpleasant feeling known as vertigo. Looking down from a height upsets the sense of balance and this gives one the sensation of falling.

March 26

WHY DO WE GET "PINS AND NEEDLES?"

"Pins and needles" is a pricking, tingling feeling in the arms or legs. It happens when we sit in one position too long, especially if we sit on one leg or lean on an arm. This pressure flattens the blood vessels and makes them swollen so the blood does not flow easily. It gives us the feeling that lots of tiny needles are being stuck into us.

When you get pins and needles it is best to rub the arm or leg, and then start moving about gently. After a little while the blood starts flowing normally and the tingling feeling disappears.

March 27

WHY DO WE NEED PHYSICAL EXERCISE?

In the old days people used to get enough exercise by doing a lot of physical work and walking long distances. Now that we travel by car or train, we walk much less. And most people do less physical work because we have machines to do many of the things men and women used to do. It is important, therefore, to find other ways to exercise our bodies. We need to use our limbs and muscles to keep the body working well. It is particularly important for children to exercise their muscles, as their bodies are still growing. So it is good to take part in sports and games, and to walk more.

March 28

WHY DOES THE HEART BEAT FASTER WHEN WE RUN?

When we run we use a lot of energy. This energy comes from burning up foods, especially fats and sugar. To convert this food into energy the body needs oxygen.

For this reason we have to breathe more deeply. The oxygen is carried to the muscles by blood. Therefore, the heart has to beat faster to do this. It is this extra flow of blood that makes our faces go red when we run. Running is very good for the heart and lungs as it helps them to work better.

However, you should make sure that you do not overdo it. If you want to take up running, or jogging, start by running a short distance at an easy pace, then gradually increase it. If you want to be an athlete, you need to do many hours of training.

March 29

WHY DO WE HAVE A SHADOW?

Rays of light, from the sun or artificial light, spread equally in all directions. When these rays of light meet a solid object, they cannot pass through it. They come to a standstill and the area behind the object is unlit. As our bodies do not let light through, we have a dark area behind us on the ground. This is called a shadow. When we move this dark area is always with us. This is why the shadow seems to move with us.

Of course, if we are walking with the light behind us, the shadow will be in front.

Perhaps you have played a game with your friends where you run and try to "catch" the shadows of your friends.

March 30 — WHY DO SOME CHILDREN WEAR GLASSES?

The human eye works like a camera lens. It projects pictures on the retina and they are carried to the brain by the optic nerve. In some people the curve of the eye is not quite normal. This means that the picture is not projected on the retina but appears in front or behind it. This causes blurred vision. Fortunately, this short- or long-sightedness can be corrected with the use of glasses (spectacles). There are also other eye problems which can be put right with glasses. To find out if you need glasses, you have to go to an optometrist (an eye doctor) and have your sight tested. You should never wear another person's glasses because they will not be suited to your particular eyesight.

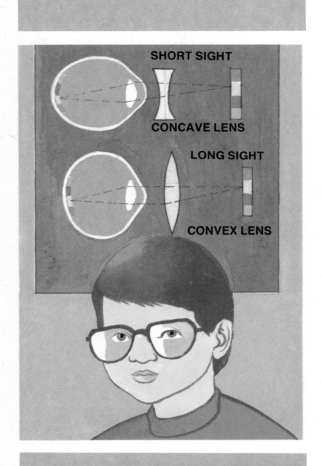

SHORT SIGHT

CONCAVE LENS

LONG SIGHT

CONVEX LENS

March 31 — WHY DOES THE SUN SOMETIMES BURN OUR SKIN?

Some sunlight is essential for the formation of our bones as children, and to

help us stay healthy and resist infection. However, if we stay in the sun too long, some of its rays can cause the skin to turn red and burn. It is better to avoid being in the sun at mid-day, which is when the sun's rays are strongest. If you do spend time in the sun you should wear a hat, and keep your skin covered. It is also advisable to put some protective cream on your skin. People who stay in the sun too long without protection not only get burned, they may also suffer from sunstroke. This makes them feel sick and is very unpleasant.

People who are born in very hot countries often have darker colored skin. This is because, thousands of years ago, their ancestors developed extra melanin – the pigment which colors the skin and gives extra protection from the harmful ultraviolet rays of the sun.

Many races in Africa, India and the Middle East wear long, loose, clothing. This not only protects them from the light, but causes movement of air under the cloth which cools the body.

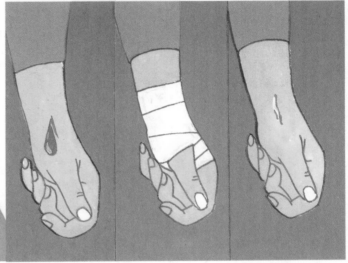

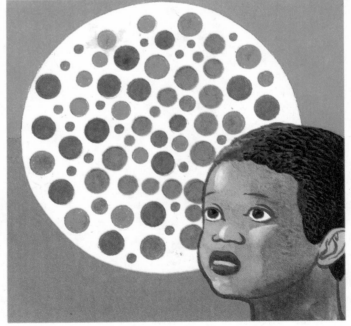

APRIL

WHY DO WE SNEEZE?

Sneezing is caused by irritation in the nose. This can be due to dust, dryness, or chemicals in the atmosphere. Pollen, from flowers, can make some people sneeze. The irritation triggers off sensitive nerve endings in the nasal passages and we experience an "explosive" sensation. The sneeze itself relieves this feeling and gets rid of the irritation.

It is polite to sneeze into a handkerchief. It is also hygienic to do that because a sneeze can be one of the first symptoms of a cold. If you do have a cold, sneezing can spread the germs.

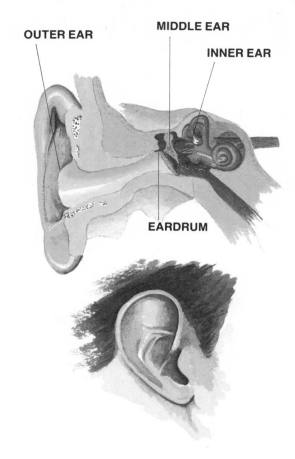

OUTER EAR   MIDDLE EAR   INNER EAR

EARDRUM

HOW DOES THE EARDRUM WORK?

The ears that you see are only part of the complicated process of hearing. The outer ear acts as a funnel which sends the sounds around us along a narrow tube. The sound waves strike against the eardrum which blocks this tube, separating it from the middle ear. Just like a drum, the eardrum vibrates and passes on the vibrations to the inner ear. A message goes to the brain which tells us what sounds we are hearing.

The eardrum and the membranes of the inner ear are very delicate so they are well protected inside the head. Even slight damage can cause some loss of hearing. This is why doctors like to treat all ear infections very quickly.

April 3 — WHY ARE WE VACCINATED?

An English doctor, Edward Jenner, discovered that people who had caught a mild illness called cowpox (because it was caught from cows) did not fall ill with the more serious illness called smallpox. He found that if he gave healthy people a serum made from the cowpox virus it would protect them from catching smallpox. The word vaccination comes from the Latin word for cow, vacca.

Vaccines have also been developed to protect people from polio, diphtheria, whooping cough, and german measles. Vaccination programs are carried out by your local doctor or clinic where all children are asked to go for injections, medicine, or pills. As a result, most of these infectious diseases are rare today.

EDWARD JENNER

April 4 — WHY DO WE SHIVER AFTER OVEREATING?

You may have experienced this peculiar sensation at some time. When food is being digested, the digestive organs need more oxygen to do the work. Therefore, more blood goes to the digestive organs. If you have eaten too much, and overloaded the system, this causes blood to be drawn from the surfaces of the body. This leads to loss of heat in the body's surface, and you react by shivering, which helps to warm you up.

April 5 — WHY DOES SKIN BRUISE WHEN WE FALL?

Below the skin are small veins which take blood to the muscles. If we fall or receive a sharp blow, some of these veins break. This causes bleeding underneath the skin and shows up as a bruise.

Bruising makes the flesh tighten and this in turn reduces the bleeding. So bruising controls the flow of blood. If much blood is

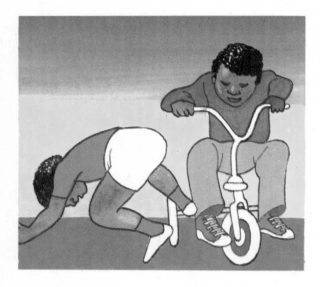

released, the bruise can be quite large and very colorful. When the bruises fade they turn a yellowish color.

Some people bruise more easily than others. It depends on how healthy they are and how sensitive their skin is.

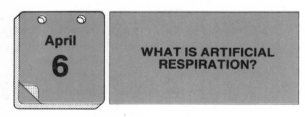

April 6

WHAT IS ARTIFICIAL RESPIRATION?

Drowning occurs when water gets into a person's breathing tubes and stops him from taking in air. This leads to lack of oxygen and the person suffocates. This

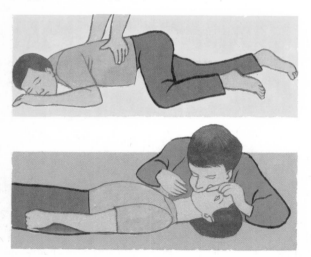

means he loses consciousness and stops breathing.

However, the heart goes on beating for some time, and breathing can start again if the person receives artificial respiration quickly. This involves either pressing on the person's chest to force out water and force in air, or mouth-to-mouth resuscitation. The rescuer should continue the artificial respiration until the victim's heart goes on beating and he continues breathing without help.

April 7

WHY DO WE WASH VEGETABLES BEFORE WE EAT THEM?

Whether we buy vegetables from shops or take them from the garden, there are often germs and small insects present. We need to remove these by washing the vegetables in clean water. Eating dirty vegetables can cause a stomach ache. It is also possible that little grubs and worms

that are sometimes found on vegetables can get into our digestive system. One such worm is called a tapeworm and it can live in our intestines.

Another reason for washing vegetables and fruit is to remove insecticides which are sprayed on them while they are growing.

April 8

WHY DO WE GET HICCUPS?

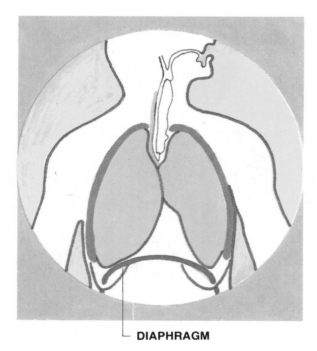

— **DIAPHRAGM**

Hiccups occur when the part of the throat containing the vocal chords suddenly tightens and closes. This stops air passing through the lungs. The feeling of having a lump in the throat occurs as the air stops. Hiccups are usually set off by an irritation of the diaphragm, which is part of the breathing system. It is a sheet of muscle separating the chest from the stomach. This irritation can be caused by gas or "wind" in the stomach, hunger, or food that is too hot.

An attack of hiccups does not last very long and does not normally need treatment.

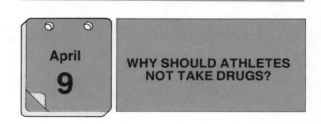

April 9

WHY SHOULD ATHLETES NOT TAKE DRUGS?

Certain drugs temporarily stimulate the muscles and make it possible for people to run faster or perform better in sports. This practice was fairly common in horse racing and greyhound racing. Now, this habit of drug-taking has extended to many other areas of athletics. It is considered a form of cheating if some athletes improve their performance by drug-taking. In the long term, it is not good for the health of the competitors. For these reasons, sports authorities in many countries have banned drug-taking and made it illegal.

April 10 — WHY DO PEOPLE GET OLD?

All living things have a certain length of life. For example, a flower starts as a bud, then blossoms, and then wilts and dies. Likewise, human beings have a limited life. Towards the end of life a person has less energy and strength. After a lifetime of work, the body naturally slows down. Hearing and eyesight may get worse, and the heart and lungs and other parts of the body do not work as well as in youth. The body gradually wears out. However, people who have had good health throughout life often remain very active in old age.

April 11 — HOW DID FLEMING DISCOVER PENICILLIN?

Penicillin, which is used to treat many infections, was discovered by Sir Alexander Fleming in 1928. While he was studying some bacteria, Fleming noticed that a fungus had somehow managed to grow on the samples of bacteria. On looking closer, he found that the fungus was actually destroying the bacteria. He realized that if it could destroy one kind it could probably destroy others. He found that the fungus contained a substance called *penicillium notatum*, which was capable of killing most of the bacteria that infect men. This is how penicillin was discovered.

SIR ALEXANDER FLEMING

April 12 — HOW DOES LIGHT CHANGE COLORS?

Color is produced by the light reflected from an object. An object can appear to change its color according to the changing light. For example, in sunlight, snow looks a brilliant white. As the sun sets, it takes on a pinkish color. When the sun has gone, the snow has a bluish tinge.

We see our surroundings according to the kind of light that is falling on them.

April 13 — WHY DO PEOPLE GO TO HEALTH SPAS?

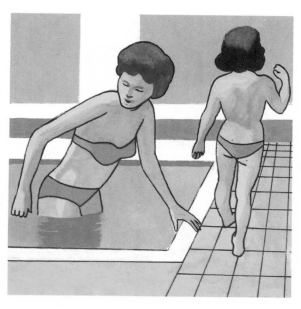

For a long time we have known that certain waters, and some mud, contain healing properties. These are known as medicinal waters. They flow from the deep layers of the earth and contain minerals which are beneficial to health. They help people with such illnesses as arthritis, and liver and nervous complaints. The water is taken in the form of drinks, baths and showers.

The places where these waters were discovered became very fashionable and were referred to as watering places or spa towns. Many people spent their holidays in these resorts. Although they are not quite so popular now, they still exist.

April 14 — WHY DO DOCTORS LOOK AT A WATCH WHEN TAKING A PULSE?

Blood is pumped through veins in the body by the heart. Large veins are called arteries. The adult heart has a regular pumping motion of about 70 beats to the minute (about 90 for a child).

When the doctor holds your wrist, he is counting the beats in the artery of your wrist. He looks at his watch so he knows when he has been counting for one minute. Then he knows what your pulse rate is. If the pulse rate is higher than normal, this is a sign that you are unwell.

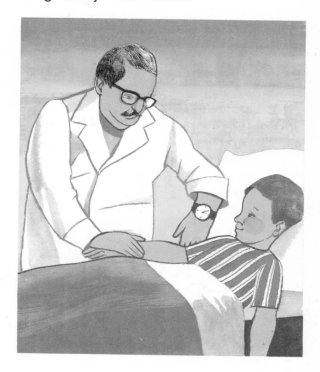

April 15 — WHY DO WE LEAN WHEN WE TRAVEL AROUND BENDS?

Whether we travel in a car or on a motorcycle the same thing happens. When the

vehicle goes around a bend in the road, the body tends to move toward the outside of the bend. To maintain balance, we then lean in the opposite direction.

The body automatically moves toward the outside of a bend or curve due to the centrifugal force. This means that anything moving around in a circle has an opposing force exerted on it.

To help us adjust to the effect of centrifugal force, the road has a slightly curved surface, known as a camber.

yourself, as you might make a mistake and pick something poisonous.

April 16

WHY DO SOME PEOPLE USE HERBAL REMEDIES?

April 17

WHY DO WOUNDS TURN INTO SCARS?

Herbs are plants which are used for improving health, or flavoring food. For thousands of years man has grown and collected plants to make medicines. Today it is possible to make them from chemicals produced in a scientific laboratory. The advantage of this is that large quantities can be produced quickly. Also, modern drugs often act faster to cure illness. However, they can cause unpleasant side effects, so many people think that the old plant remedies are better for the body.

You should never experiment with plants

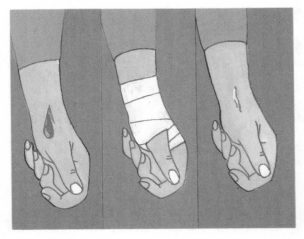

Our bodies have a natural ability to heal themselves. So if you cut yourself, your body immediately reacts by producing new tissue and making protective cover for the blood vessels. This layer of granular tissue protects the wound from infection while the healing process is taking place. When the wound is healed, the top layer dries up, forming a scab. When the wound is completely healed, the scab falls off, as it is no longer needed. A mark is left and this is called a scar. If it is only a shallow cut, the scar will usually disappear. A deeper wound may leave a permanent scar.

LIVER

STOMACH

GALL BLADDER

April 18

WHY DO SOME PEOPLE GET STONES IN THEIR BODIES?

Stones, or gallstones, are made up of various minerals. They form in the gall bladder. It is thought that they are caused by faulty functioning of the liver. Because these stones, or granules, are often rough or sharp, they can cause pain.

People who have these stones usually have to drink a lot of water to flush them out of their system. If they cannot be flushed out, they may have to be removed surgically.

April 19

WHY DOES THE DOCTOR TAP A PATIENT'S KNEECAP?

The doctor taps a patient's kneecap to find out if his nervous system is working well. Normally, when the knee is tapped, either with a small hammer or the hand, the leg jerks out. This is called a reflex action. So when the doctor does this he is testing reflexes.

If there is no reaction to this test (if the leg does not move), this may be a sign that there is some damage. This damage may be in the spine or in the nerves of the leg.

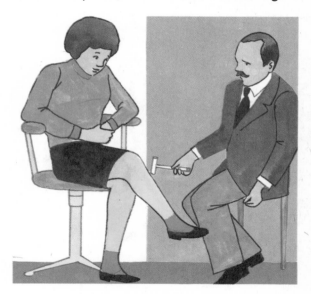

April 20

WHY DO WE TAKE PILLS WHEN WE ARE IN PAIN?

Pain is the body's way of telling us that something is wrong. So it is a signal that we need help. However, once we have had

Some people have a weakness in their eyes which causes one eye to move in a different direction from the other. It is usually called a "lazy" eye, or a squint. Some cases can be corrected with glasses. Special eye exercises can also help people who suffer from squinting.

One kind of squinting, called "paralyzed squinting," causes the person to lose all sense of distance. This makes it difficult for those people to take part in some sports. It also means that it would be unsafe for them to drive a car or any other vehicle.

April
22

WHAT IS COLOR BLINDNESS?

treatment for the illness or accident, we can do something about the pain. There are pills we can take which soothe the nervous system, so we no longer feel the pain. You should only take pills given to you by your doctor or parents.

April
21

WHY DO SOME PEOPLE'S EYES SEEM TO MOVE IN DIFFERENT DIRECTIONS?

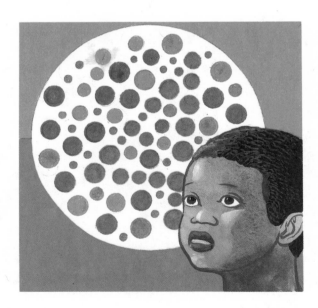

People who are color-blind cannot tell the difference between one color and another. For example, the colors red, green and yellow are seen as different shades of gray. Some people may see red as green. This is obviously very inconvenient for them as they are unable to pick out the correct colors of traffic lights and therefore cannot get a driver's licence.

This condition was first studied by an English chemist, John Dalton, who was himself color-blind. This is why color-blindness is known, in medical terms, as Daltonism. The illustration shows a test card for color blindness.

WHY DO WE GET CAVITIES IN TEETH?

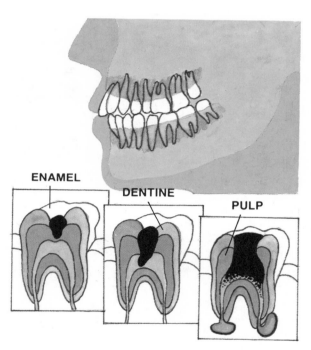

ENAMEL   DENTINE   PULP

Tooth decay is caused by a build-up of bits of food, saliva and bacteria on the tooth. This produces an acid which eats into the enamel of the tooth, then the inner layer, or dentine. Finally, the pulpy part in the middle of the tooth is affected. This is where the nerves are, so this is where the pain comes from.

There are several things you can do to prevent tooth decay. Firstly, you should clean your teeth regularly. Secondly, you should have a healthy diet and avoid eating too many sweets, as sugar helps form the acid that makes holes in teeth. Thirdly, you should go to your dentist frequently. Fluoride in drinking water also helps prevent tooth decay.

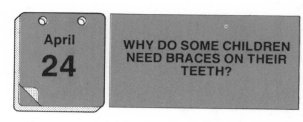

WHY DO SOME CHILDREN NEED BRACES ON THEIR TEETH?

Humans are able to grow two sets of teeth. One set grows during the first few years of life. Then at about the age of 6 children start to lose their first teeth and the second teeth grow in their place. Some children's second teeth come in crooked, or sticking out, and their dentist may decide they need braces to help straighten them. They may be strips of wire fastened around several teeth, or metal plates to hold each tooth in place.

Straight teeth not only look more attractive, but are more efficient at chewing food, so it is worth wearing your braces if the dentist prescribes them.

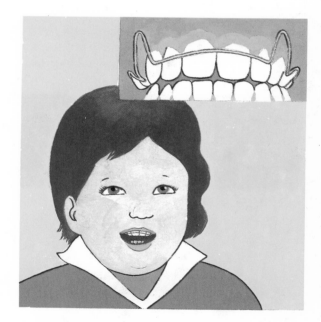

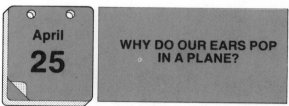

WHY DO OUR EARS POP IN A PLANE?

When we go up in an airplane, or up a mountain, there is a change in the pressure of the atmosphere. This change in altitude

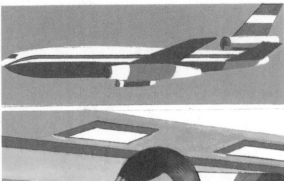

The practice of mummifying, or preserving, bodies for burial was common in ancient Egypt. It was done mainly for religious reasons. After the internal organs were removed, the body was soaked in various spices, oils, and salts and wrapped in linen bandages. This process prevented the corpse from decaying.

Tribes in South America and other parts of the world used similar methods to preserve dead bodies.

In Egypt the bodies were placed in tombs called pyramids. The tombs of the rulers (Pharaohs) were very ornate and contained many precious items.

Naturally preserved mummies have been discovered in Scandinavian peat bogs.

and atmospheric pressure disturbs the tissue in the ear. This is why we experience a popping sensation. This feeling goes if we swallow several times. Some airlines give passengers sweets to suck, as the sucking action helps to relieve pressure in the ear.

April 27

WHY DO SOME MEN GROW BEARDS?

April 26

WHY ARE BODIES MUMMIFIED?

Men produce a hormone (body chemical) which enables them to grow hair on the lower part of their faces. This will grow into a moustache and beard if it is not shaved off. As early as the Iron Age men have chosen to shave, or to shape their beards and moustaches to improve the way they look. They have also shaved for comfort in a warm climate – beards can be hot and itchy! Because the razors they used were open blades, they were quite difficult and dangerous to use. Nowadays, with safety and electric razors available, more men choose to be clean shaven.

April 28

WOULD OUR BODIES BE MORE DURABLE IF THEY WERE MADE OF STEEL?

Steel is a wonderful material for many products, but is not as flexible and durable as the human body. Although steel is very hard it doesn't have much movement. If the human body were made of steel it would wear out in many places long before flesh

and bones. We are very fortunate in having a body which has the power to heal itself and renew its cells and tissues.

So, although a robot is an amazing piece of machinery, it is not nearly as strong and clever as a human being. However, doctors may use metals and plastics in surgery. Artificial parts can replace a damaged part of the body, such as a hip joint.

April 29

WHY DON'T WE ALL HAVE THE SAME COLOR HAIR?

Melanin, a brown pigment which gives color to skin, also gives color to hair. Because some people have more melanin, they have darker hair. Hair colors range from blond to black. People who have a shortage of pigment have very pale skin, hair and eyes. They are known as albinos.

Old people have gray hair because as the body gets older it produces less melanin, so the natural hair color fades.

WHY CAN PEOPLE FLOAT EASILY IN THE DEAD SEA?

You may have noticed that it is easier to float in the sea than in a swimming pool. This is because the sea water which is salty and therefore more dense, makes you more buoyant (able to float).

The Dead Sea, a lake between Israel and Jordan, is very salty, containing about 275 grams (6 ounces) of salt per liter (per pint). This enables people to float on the surface without having to swim. Of course, it is not very pleasant if you accidentally swallow some of the water.

Because the water of the Dead Sea is so salty it cannot support any vegetable or animal life, apart from bacteria.

MAY

Green plants owe their color to a pigment called chlorophyll. This substance absorbs sunlight. It converts this light energy into chemical energy, which is stored in the plant and released as oxygen. It is this process, called photosynthesis, that supplies the atmosphere with most of its oxygen. Without green plants, there would be no life on Earth.

If you have plants in the house, it is important to make sure they are in a position where they will get sunlight.

The leafy parts of plants consist largely of water. Some of this is lost as the plant breathes and some dries out in the sun. This water has to be replaced by water drawn up through the plant's roots. Minerals the plant needs from the soil are dissolved in the water, so this is how the plant is fed. These minerals are particularly important to green plants because they are needed for the process of photosynthesis.

Sunlight is essential to keep plants and trees green and healthy. The surface of green plants and the leaves of trees have to be exposed to sunlight so that photosynthesis can take place. Trees which grow in woods or forests make a lot of shade. Therefore, to obtain the light they need, they grow upward towards the sunlight. New branches and leaves grow on the upper part of the tree where there is maximum light. House plants tend to lean toward the light for the same reason.

Some of the tallest trees in the world are found in tropical jungles. This is because these areas have long periods of sunlight and a lot of rain. This abundance of light and water (which feeds the trees with minerals from the soil) produces very rapid growth throughout the year.

May 3

WHY DO PEOPLE PUT MANURE ON THE GROUND?

If land is being used all the time for growing crops and vegetables, the minerals in the soil get used up and need replacing. Farmers and gardeners put fertilizer on the ground to replenish the soil with all the nutrients plants need.

There are two types of fertilizer – mineral and organic. The mineral fertilizers are manufactured and can be bought. The organic fertilizers are made of plant matter and animal dung built up over a period of time into a manure heap. Farmers spread this manure onto the earth.

Animal dung is waste products from digested food and contains nutrients which are easily absorbed through the roots of plants. It is best to spread it over the ground when it is fresh so that none of the nutritional value is lost. Sometimes the manure is dampened so that it soaks into the ground more quickly and easily.

May 5 — WHY DO SOME TREES LOSE THEIR LEAVES IN WINTER?

Each leaf on a tree has a limited life, depending on the type of tree and the climate. In a moderate climate, most trees lose their leaves in the fall and grow new leaves in the spring.

These trees are called deciduous trees. They lose their leaves in the fall because there is less sunlight and a lower temperature. This slows down the chemical activity produced by photosynthesis. Therefore, the leaves fade and fall off the trees.

If there are strong winds in the fall, the trees lose their leaves more quickly.

However, some trees remain green all through the year. These are called evergreens. The leaves on evergreen trees have a longer life than those on deciduous trees. Because they remain green and do not all die at the same time, the tree is green all the year. As each leaf dies it is replaced by another one.

May 6 — WHY DO THE LEAVES OF SOME TREES CHANGE COLOR IN THE FALL?

Green leaves contain a pigment called chlorophyll that gives them a green color. During the fall, when there is less sunlight and the temperature is lower, the chlorophyll changes and disappears. Then yellow and orange pigments, known as carotenes, become visible. The leaves gradually change from green through a range of orange/red shades to yellow. Then they dry up and drop from the tree. The changing colors of the trees in the fall make the countryside very beautiful.

May 7 — WHY DO TREE TRUNKS HAVE CIRCLES IN THEM?

When a tree is cut down, you can see a number of dark circles in the wood which get smaller toward the center. The older the tree, the more circles there are. A tree grows much more in the spring and summer than in fall and winter. Within the

trunk is a ring of cells. As the tree grows, the cells increase. The woody cells that are produced in spring and summer appear as light-colored rings. When the growth slows down in colder months, the wood hardens and becomes darker. So one year's growth is marked by this dark ring. By counting the number of dark rings it is possible to work out how old the tree is.

May 8

WHY DO WE GRAFT TREES?

Some trees produce a large quantity of excellent fruits, but the tree itself may not be very strong. In this case, a branch from the fruit tree can be grafted onto the trunk of another, stronger tree. This is done by placing the branch in a prepared split in the trunk of the stronger tree. In time, the branch will grow and produce other branches, and eventually fruit. This way, the best qualities of both trees are combined. Grafting is also done to reproduce trees that have become rare or diseased.

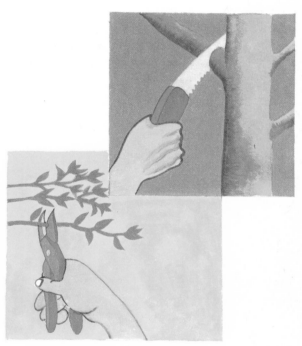

May 9

WHY DO PEOPLE CUT OFF BRANCHES OF TREES?

Cutting some of the branches off trees and bushes is called pruning. One reason for pruning is to remove dead or diseased wood. This keeps the tree healthy and encourages growth. In the case of a fruit tree, pruning helps to produce larger fruit as the nutrients are not wasted in feeding unnecessary branches. People also prune rose bushes in order to grow larger flowers. Ornamental trees and bushes are pruned to give them a more attractive shape.

May 10

WHY DO TREES NEAR THE SEA GROW AT AN ANGLE?

Sometimes trees which grow near the sea seem to grow at an angle and appear to lean.

This is because from the time they are young (saplings) they are blown by very strong winds from the sea. Because young trees bend easily, the strength of the wind makes them grow at a slant instead of upright. As the trees mature, the trunks harden at this angle. The trees, therefore, grow permanently slanted.

ALMOND BLOSSOM

May 11

WHY DO FLOWERS GROW ON TREES?

The flower is the part of a plant which produces seeds. These seeds then produce more plants. The flower is the reproductive part of the plant.

In the case of trees, the flower (or blossom) grows into fruit or berries. It is the fruit or berries which hold the seeds. If you cut open a fruit or berry, you will see the seeds inside.

Some trees have flowers which are hardly noticeable as they are very small or are the same color as the leaves. Other trees have very obvious and beautiful blossoms, such as the almond tree. However, with the almond tree, the fruit is the nut and the inner part of the almond, the kernel (which is the part we eat) is the seed.

WHY IS THERE A HOLE IN THE BOTTOM OF A FLOWER POT?

WHY DO LEAVES HAVE VEINS?

Plants in the house give people pleasure, especially if there is no garden. But house plants do require a lot of care. The reason they are planted in pots with a hole in the bottom is to allow water to drain through. If there is too much water in the pot, the plant becomes waterlogged. Plants can die from having too much water just as they can die from lack of water.

The hole at the bottom of the pot also allows air to circulate. If there were no air in the earth, the plants might suffocate. A layer of pebbles in the bottom of the pot also helps to drain and aerate the plant. When roots appear through the hole, the plant needs repotting.

The water and minerals that a tree or plant needs to keep it healthy are absorbed from the soil through the roots. These nutrients, which are the plant's food, then have to be taken to every part of the plant.

The liquid which carries nutrients through plants and trees is called sap. The circulation of the sap is similar to the circulation of blood in the human body. The sap is carried by capillary vessels, or veins. When the veins arrive at the edges of leaves, they branch out and get narrower so that every part of the leaf is nourished. These veins make a very attractive pattern on the surface of the leaves.

WHY DO SOME FLOWERS CLOSE UP AT NIGHT?

WHY DO FLOWERS DROOP?

Some flowers are very delicate and are sensitive to changes in temperature and light. So at dusk, when it gets cooler and the light begins to fade, these flowers close up their petals as if they were going to sleep. It is not absolutely certain if it is lack of light or the drop in temperature which causes this closing of the petals, or a combination of both. Sometimes, when it becomes very hot during the day, the flowers close their petals to protect themselves from the heat.

Flowers, like all living things, have a limited life. As time goes on, they begin to fade, wither, and droop. Once the flower has been fertilized the petals and stamens decay and fall off, leaving the seed pod.

If a flower has been cut from its root, it withers earlier as the supply of sap has been cut off. However, cut flowers can be kept alive for several days in water.

It is possible to extract the scent of the flower because it dissolves in greasy liquids. The flowers are soaked in a greasy substance which absorbs the scent. This substance is then heated and the vapor is condensed (turned into liquid) by cooling. This liquid is then collected and used as a perfume in different products. Perfumes can also be made artificially by means of chemicals.

May 16 — WHY ARE SOME FLOWERS SCENTED?

It is through the flower that many plants reproduce themselves. This becomes possible when the ovule is fertilized by pollen and a seed is formed. The pollen is often transferred to the ovule by bees and insects. It is the scent or color of the flower which attracts the insects. This scent is necessary for fertilization.

Some plants are pollinated by the wind. Others reproduce themselves by sending up shoots from their roots or tubers. These plants, therefore, do not need a scent to attract insects.

May 17 — HOW ARE FLOWERS MADE INTO PERFUMES?

The scents of different flowers are used in the manufacture of perfume, cologne, soap, talcum powder, and other toiletries.

May 18 — HOW DO FLOWERS GET THEIR DIFFERENT COLORS?

Nature has given us many different varieties of flowers in different colors. The colors in flowers come from different pigments. Chlorophyll is the pigment which makes leaves green. Likewise the petals of flowers have pigments to make them different colors. For example, the pigment which gives an orange color is called carotene. Some petals have more than one color and this is because they contain different types of pigment. Colors may fade or change as the flower gets older.

As the fruit ripens, different pigments are formed and these change the color of the fruit. Of course some fruits are green even when ripe, such as greengages and certain types of apples.

If fruit falls off a tree before it is completely ripe, it can be placed on a sunny window ledge to ripen behind the glass. Green tomatoes can also be left to ripen in this way.

May 20

WHY DO WE CALL GREEN GRAPES WHITE GRAPES?

There are two kinds of grapes: the green ones which are used to make white wine, and the purple ones which are used to make red wine.

We refer to the green ones as white grapes to distinguish them from the others, although of course they are really a greenish yellow color when ripe. We call the dark purple or red ones black grapes. This marks the contrast between them.

The grapes used for wine are cultivated especially for wine-making. The ones we eat are called dessert grapes.

May 19

WHY SHOULD WE ONLY EAT FRUIT WHEN IT IS RIPE?

When some fruit is green it is not yet ripe. If you eat unripe fruit you may have an upset stomach. Unripe fruit is not only difficult to digest but it also has a sour taste and is usually very hard. So it is better to leave the fruit on the tree or bush until it has ripened.

WHY ARE GRAPES AND OTHER FRUITS SPRAYED?

All kinds of fruit attract insects that feed off the fruit and spoil it for human consumption. As farmers cannot sell spoiled fruit, they do everything they can to stop the insects settling on the fruit.

One way of getting rid of insects is to spray the fruit with a chemical insecticide. Until recently insecticide was sprayed onto the fruit by a hand pump. The pump was carried on the back of the farm worker and he sprayed the insecticide onto the fruit with a hand-held dispenser. Of course this took a long time as the farm workers had to walk many miles around the farm or vineyard. Now there are special machines which do the work much more quickly and effectively. On very large farms and estates, light aircraft may be used for the spraying.

It is important to wash fruit before eating it in order to remove traces of insecticide.

WHY DO WE MAKE JUICE FROM FRUIT?

Fruit is a very good source of vitamins, especially vitamin C. This is the vitamin we need to help us resist infections, and for good hair, teeth and bones. Fruit is also pleasant to eat, being a naturally sweet food.

Fruit farmers grow more fresh fruit than we could eat, and much of it is used to make drinks that will keep in cartons or bottles for a long time. Orange, lemon, grape, apple, and other juices can be bought in this form.

In the past, when fruit could not be refrigerated or preserved any other way, grape and apple juice were fermented into wine and cider. This would keep for a long time without going bad. These drinks are still popular with adults today.

May 23

WHAT IS THE DIFFERENCE BETWEEN BLACK AND GREEN OLIVES?

Olives grow mainly in countries with a hot climate. Some olives are picked before they are ripe when they are still green. They cannot be eaten raw as they contain a substance which makes them very bitter. So they are processed to remove the bitterness. In some countries they use a process which darkens green olives and makes them look black. In other countries they pick the ripe olives which are naturally black.

May 24

HOW ARE OLIVES MADE INTO OIL?

Olives that are used to make oil are picked when they are ripe and black in color. The olives are put in a press and ground to squeeze out the oil. This is called the first pressing and this oil is the best quality. Further pressings of the olives produce an oil which is edible but is not considered quite so good.

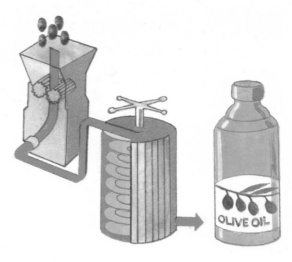

Olive oil is used in salads and for cooking. In Mediterranean countries this oil is a very important ingredient in many dishes.

May 25

HOW IS RICE GROWN?

Rice is a kind of grass. Because it likes both heat and water it can only be grown easily in tropical climates, such as in China, India, Indonesia, Africa, and South America, where it is an important food.

Rice has to be planted in mud, and the water level in paddy (rice) fields kept the same all the time. These fields are often made on the sides of hills, in terraces. The water drains down from one field to another, keeping the fields wet. Before pumps were available the water had to be carried in tin cans to the top of the hill.

May 26 — WHY DOES WOOD BURN?

Trees, like other living things, possess two essential elements: carbon and hydrogen. With the help of oxygen in the air, both these elements burn easily when set alight. In primitive times wood was man's main source of light and heat. Fire was also used to scare wild animals away. People would set fire to wood by rubbing two stones together to make a spark.

Now, although we have other sources of fuel, it is still very pleasant to sit by a log fire in the winter.

May 27 — HOW IS CHARCOAL MADE?

Charcoal is a man-made product, so it is not found in mines like coal.

It is made by the incomplete burning of wood. This is done by piling up branches of wood of the same size and covering them with a dome of earth, then setting fire to them. The earth reduces the amount of oxygen around the wood, which allows the wood to burn very slowly. In this way the

central piece of each branch becomes charred, and this forms the charcoal.

May 28 — WHY DO POTATOES HAVE "EYES?"

You will have noticed that the surface of a potato often has little holes and bumps, which we call "eyes." The eye forms the bud of young shoots which, if left in the earth, would grow into new potato plants. The shoot would grow from the food reserves in the potato. In this way, the potato reproduces itself.

If an old potato is left for a long time little shoots start to grow from it. This sometimes happens when it is left in a vegetable rack.

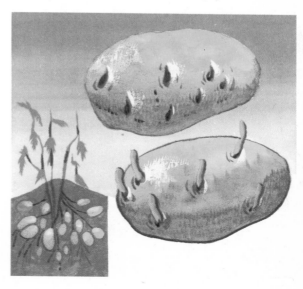

May 29

HOW DO SOME PLANTS GROW UP WALLS?

Plants that grow up walls are known as climbers. They have small moving parts known as tendrils, suckers, and hooks, that enable them to cling to the wall, or other surfaces.

These climbing plants are often used to cover walls, fences, and the walls of houses to make them more attractive.

May 30

WHY DO NETTLES STING?

On the surface of nettle leaves there are little hairs which carry a poisonous liquid. If we touch a nettle leaf, these delicate little hairs will break off and pierce the skin, releasing their liquid. This is what causes the stinging sensation and causes the skin to redden. However, the liquid is only slightly poisonous and the irritation soon goes. Many people rub nettle stings with a dock leaf as they find that this has a soothing effect on them. Fortunately, dock leaves can usually be found growing near nettles.

WHY DO WE CRY WHEN WE PEEL ONIONS?

Onions contain a substance which is rich in sulphur. When we peel and chop onions, the vapor is released and causes irritation to the eyes. This makes the eyes water, so it appears as if we are crying. Shedding tears in these circumstances is a natural way of protecting the eyes from harmful substances. The tears wash the eyes and dissolve any irritating or harmful substance, making it less concentrated. A piece of grit in the eye also produces tears, which then wash away the grit and soothe the eye.

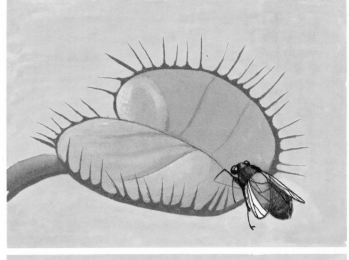

JUNE

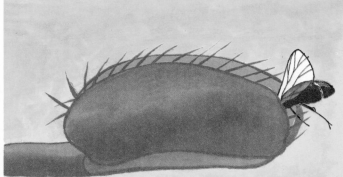

WHY ARE PLANTS SUCH AS WHEAT AND BARLEY KNOWN AS CEREALS?

The word cereals comes from the name of the Roman goddess, Ceres. She was the goddess of the growth of food plants and the protectress of agriculture, the equivalent of the Greek goddess Demeter.

Ceres is pictured wearing a crown made of ears of corn. A festival was held in her honor known as Cerealia. During this festival impressive circus acts were performed and bread was distributed to the poor.

WHEAT

WHEAT   **BARLEY**   **RYE**

June 2

WHY IS WASTE PAPER RECYCLED?

Paper is mostly made from wood pulp. The wood comes from quick-growing forests which have to be specially planted, felled, and transported to the paper mills. It is easier and more economical to collect up suitable waste paper, such as old

newspaper and cardboard boxes and re-use them. When it has been washed, pulped, and re-rolled the paper is not very white, but is quite suitable for brown or colored papers.

June 3

WHY DO SOME PLANTS HAVE BERRIES?

The flower of some plants is the reproductive part. In some cases the flower develops into a pod or berry. It is the berry which contains the seeds. The berries drop to the ground and some of the seeds sprout. Birds also help to spread the seeds by plucking the berries and taking them away to eat them. Some of the seeds are dispersed as they drop to the ground while the bird is eating the berry. Some berries,

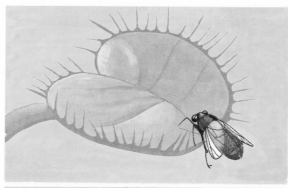

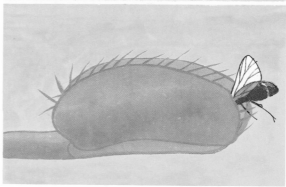

such as blackberries, are eaten by human beings, but others may be poisonous. So you shouldn't eat berries unless you are sure they are edible.

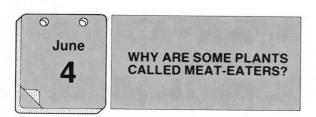

June
4

WHY ARE SOME PLANTS CALLED MEAT-EATERS?

Most plants are fed through their roots with water which has dissolved in it the salts and minerals the plants need. However, some plants have developed another way of getting food which enables them to live in places that provide very little nutrition from the soil. These plants are able to trap and feed on insects. Some have tentacles coated with a glue-like substance to which the insect sticks. Others have a kind of trapdoor containing little hairs. When the insect touches these hairs, the trapdoor closes and captures it. All these plants have special digestive enzymes to absorb the insects.

June
5

WHY ARE CAMPFIRES DANGEROUS IN FORESTS?

During the summer we often hear news of forest fires. Thousands of acres of trees in woods and forests are burned every year in France alone, and it takes over 20 years for young trees to take their place. Not only

are the trees lost, but hundreds of birds, animals and insects may be killed.

The problem is that fire spreads quickly from one tree to another, especially if there is any wind. One of the best ways to stop these fires spreading is to dig fire trenches about 60 meters/180 feet wide at intervals through the forests so that when the wind blows, fire cannot travel across the gap.

June 6

WHY DOES COFFEE KEEP US AWAKE?

Coffee comes from the coffee bean, a plant which originated in Ethiopia, but is now grown in many parts of the world. The main ingredient of coffee is caffeine, a substance which stimulates the nervous system and the muscular tissue. It relieves tiredness and makes us feel more alert mentally. If we drink it just before going to bed, it is likely to keep us awake. So it is better not to drink coffee in the evening.

When coffee manufacturers became aware that some people wanted to drink it without the stimulating effect, they started producing a coffee which had most of the caffeine removed artificially. This is called decaffeinated coffee.

June 7

WHY DO PEOPLE BUILD GREENHOUSES?

Many plants thrive only when the temperature and humidity of their environment remain the same. In some climates, it is not possible to grow certain plants outdoors because of the changing conditions. The greenhouse was designed to create and maintain the right conditions for such plants. This means that exotic plants can be grown even in cold climates. Gardeners use greenhouses to grow such things as grapes and tomatoes, as well as exotic flowers. Greenhouses also provide good conditions for starting off new plants, which are later transferred to the garden.

June 8

WHY SHOULD WE CUT FLOWERS AFTER SUNSET?

Sap is to flowers what blood is to the human being. The sap circulates in the plant in a similar way to the blood in the human body. But the perspiration of a plant is a little more complicated. It depends on light and temperature. During the day, therefore, there is a lot more activity in the plant. When the sun sets, this activity dies down. This is a good time to pick flowers as the pores of the plant will be closed, so the petals will retain their moisture longer.

June 9

WHY IS THE USE OF INSECTICIDES CONTROLLED?

Chemical insecticides have been used for many years. But from 1945, the discovery of DDT and other similar

insecticides made their use much more effective and widespread. It was found that even plagues of insects could be controlled.

However, it was later found that the harmful elements of these insecticides were retained in the earth and absorbed by plants and animals. When people ate fruit, vegetables, meat and animal products, these chemicals were transferred and stored in their bodies. Because of this, health authorities became concerned and restrictions were imposed on the use of insecticides.

Nevertheless, it is still advisable to thoroughly wash all fruit, vegetables and salad ingredients before eating them.

June 10

WHY IS THE NAME LINNAEUS ASSOCIATED WITH PLANTS?

Although many well-known men in the past had made studies of plants, it was not until the eighteenth century that a scientific study was made. This was done by a Swedish naturalist called Carl von

CARL VON LINNE

Linne, who published his work under the Latin version of his name, Linnaeus. He divided all plants into families, or species, and worked out a system of names. Many plants are still known by these names. He was also famous for his work on the reproduction of plants. By studying their stamens, he was able to describe how plants reproduce themselves. His work was extremely useful to botanists.

June 11

DO PLANTS SLEEP AT NIGHT?

Even plants sleep, not because they are tired and need to recover as we do, but because there is no light at night.

Plants need sunlight for life and growth. When the sun is shining the heads of the flowers open up to receive as much of the energy as possible. When the sun sets the flowerheads close to avoid heat loss. You can prove this if you take a plant from a warm, light room into a cold, dark one. The petals will close up. Back in the warmth they will open again.

June 12

WHY IS IT DANGEROUS TO PICK MUSHROOMS?

Mushrooms belong to the fungus family of plants. Unlike most plants, they do not need light to grow; in fact some mushrooms spring up overnight. The toadstool is also a kind of mushroom, but it is poisonous and can cause death or serious illness. This is why we have to be very careful when we pick mushrooms. It is safer to buy them from a store.

If you see something that looks like mushrooms growing in a field don't pick them unless you are with an adult who knows the difference between mushrooms and toadstools.

June 13

WHY ARE THE TOPS OF MOUNTAINS SO BARE?

Most plants need a rich soil, warm temperature and good drainage. On high hills or mountains the soil is poorer and the temperature lower, so only certain hardy plants can grow at these heights. This is

why valleys and low-lying plains are greener than mountainous country.

Scientists who study the soil have discovered which plants grow well in certain conditions. They have also drawn up tables which show the stages or "steps" of vegetation, and which plants grow at each level.

June 14

WHY DOES MIMOSA SHRINK WHEN YOU TOUCH IT?

Mimosa, like other plants of its kind, shrinks and temporarily withers at the slightest touch. Until recently this strange behavior was a source of surprise to many people and of great curiosity to the naturalist. Modern science, however, has managed to clear up this mystery. It has been discovered that mimosa, like all plants can actually *feel*. It is now possible to record not only the sensitivity of plants but their "moments of happiness" and also their "sufferings." This means we should take great care of plants.

June 15

HOW DO WE GET RUBBER FROM TREES?

Rubber comes from a tropical tree. The juice of the rubber tree, called latex, is extracted through slanting cuts in the bark. The juice drips into a container attached to the tree. It is then collected and made into rubber, which can be used for car tires, boots, etc.

Another juice extracted from trees is maple syrup. It comes from the maple tree which is grown in North America. The juice flows out of holes bored into the wood of the tree. Maple syrup is popular in the U.S.A. and is used on pancakes and ice cream.

June 16

HOW WAS THE HABIT OF SMOKING TOBACCO INTRODUCED?

Tobacco was discovered by Europeans in the 16th century when explorers, such as Christopher Columbus, visited Central America. They noticed that the natives, the American Indians, smoked tobacco,

soil produces further growth. This shows how sunlight and warmth can increase the growth of plants.

June
18

WHAT IS
CROP ROTATION?

thinking that it had medical properties. It was also used in Indian ceremonies, such as smoking the pipe of peace. Jean Nicot, French ambassador to Portugal, introduced it to his country, claiming that it could cure headaches. The tobacco plant was named *nicotinia* after him, and the substance nicotine, found in tobacco, also got its name from him.

Now, of course, tobacco is known to be harmful to the health and smoking is discouraged, especially among young, growing people.

Different crops take different nutrients from the soil and give back different elements when their remains are ploughed back into the ground. If one kind of plant is grown in the same field year after year, the soil may become short of some nutrients. If one crop is planted one year and another the next and so on, results are better. This is crop rotation. Sometimes nothing is planted in a field so that the soil gets a rest. This is referred to as a fallow field.

June
17

WHY IS THERE SO MUCH
FOLIAGE IN TROPICAL
FORESTS?

In tropical areas, around the equator, there are very high temperatures. This means there is a high rate of evaporation and therefore high rainfall. The rain encourages the rapid growth of plants and trees. As the fruits and leaves fall to the ground and decompose, they provide nutrients for the soil. This richness of the

June 19 — HOW LONG CAN A CACTUS LIVE WITHOUT WATER?

Plants such as cacti can survive in the desert for several years without rain. They need water just like any other plant, but have become adapted to a dry environment. They don't have leaves, which lose water rapidly in the heat. Their thick stems act as containers or reservoirs to store water against drought (when there is no rain for long periods.) Also, the cactus has wide, shallow roots, extending for a great distance around them, to trap as much rain as possible from the occasional storms.

If you have cactus plants at home they will survive even if you forget to water them for several weeks; but if you want them to grow and flower they will need some water and plant food.

June 20 — WHAT IS SANDALWOOD USED FOR?

Sandalwood trees are found in south-eastern Asia and the islands of the South Pacific. These trees have been cultivated

for centuries and form an important part in the economy and traditions of those countries. The yellowish wood of the sandalwood tree is very fragrant and is used to make incense. This incense is used in eastern funeral ceremonies and religious rites. The scented oil of the tree is used in perfumes, soap, and candles and the wood is made into ornamental boxes and furniture.

June 21 — WHY DO WE PLANT TREES IN CITIES?

Because there are many people living and working in cities, vast amounts of oxygen are consumed. At the same time, a lot of waste matter is released into the atmosphere by cars and industry. So the air in towns and cities is not very pure.

Trees and plants give out oxygen; so by planting trees and creating parks in our cities we can replace the oxygen consumed and purify the atmosphere.

June 22

WHY ARE SOME GARDENS CALLED BOTANICAL GARDENS?

Private and public gardens and parks are created to make our surroundings more pleasant. The purpose of botanical gardens is to provide the right setting for making a scientific study of different kinds of plants. Botanical gardens contain greenhouses which enable exotic plants to be grown. There are also laboratories for study and experiments and libraries.

Botanical gardens are usually open to the public, so we are given the opportunity to see plants which we wouldn't normally see in our own country. One of the most famous is Kew Gardens in England where you can see a wide variety of plants and trees from many countries.

June 23

WHY ARE INSECTS ATTRACTED TO CERTAIN FLOWERS?

Flowers are fertilized by pollen and the pollen is often transferred to the ovule (to make the seed) by insects. The bright colors and scent of the flowers attract the insects.

There is a type of orchid which looks so much like the female of certain insects that the male insect is attracted to it and tries to mate with it. Of course, in doing this the insect pollinates and fertilizes the flower. So we can see that the shape, color, and scent of flowers are not just accidental; they have a very specific purpose.

June 24

WHY DOES SOME WOOD SINK IN WATER?

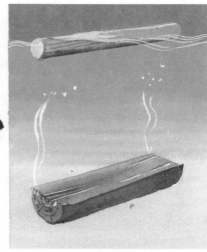

Many types of wood are very light and porous and able to float on water. However, some kinds of wood are dense and sink if dropped in water. This is the case with ebony, which possesses a density greater than water, so it sinks. The ebony tree grows in the tropics. Its exceptionally hard wood can be very highly polished, so it is often used for cabinet-making, knife handles, and black piano keys.

CYPRESS
OLIVE

LOTUS   TULIP   ROSE

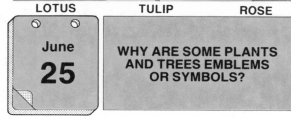

June 25

WHY ARE SOME PLANTS AND TREES EMBLEMS OR SYMBOLS?

Since ancient times trees and plants have been associated with events in the life of man. The cypress tree is a symbol of death and mourning. The olive tree represents peace. In the Bible story of Noah and his ark, a dove bore an olive leaf to him, indicating that the flood had subsided. Even now we use the phrase "to extend an olive branch," meaning to make peace.

The lotus flower is considered sacred by some eastern countries. Other flowers which have become emblems are the tulip, associated with Holland, and the rose which is the emblem of England.

June 26

WHY IS THE CULTIVATION OF CERTAIN PLANTS CONTROLLED?

Many plants have medicinal value and are made into drugs which are used to relieve pain and help the healing process. However, some of these substances can be harmful. One such substance is opium, which is found in a type of poppy in eastern countries. Uncontrolled use of such drugs without medical supervision has harmful effects, not only on the individual's health but also on society. This is why governments enforce strict rules about the growing of such plants.

June 27 — WHY DO SOME TREES HAVE SPECIAL MEANING?

Just as we have special feelings for some people, we may also have good feelings about trees and objects which have pleasant memories for us. Many trees have historical interest because of events associated with them. In England the oak tree has special significance and has many royal associations. Charles II hid in an oak tree after his defeat at Worcester. The "parliament oak" in Sherwood Forest is the tree under which Edward I held a parliament. In Windsor Great Park there is "William the Conqueror's Oak." In Mexico there is the "tree of the sad knight," where Cortes wept about his defeat at Otumba.

June 28 — WHY DO WE USE THE PHRASE "TURNIP HEAD?"

This phrase may be used jokingly in families when someone is behaving stupidly. It means that the person isn't being very intelligent and has a head like a turnip. Sometimes, however, calling a person by the name of a vegetable can be meant affectionately. For example, in France people may refer to someone as *mon petit chou* (my little cabbage), using the phrase as a term of endearment.

June 29 — WHY IS IT IMPORTANT TO LOOK AFTER FORESTS?

Forests are very important to the environment. Firstly, they play a vital part in maintaining the balance of nature, since the leaves of trees keep the air supplied with oxygen and provide moisture which gives us rain. Secondly, trees play an important part in everyday life, as wood is used for house building, paper making, fuel, and in many other ways.

Forests can deteriorate through fire, too much tree-felling, plagues of insects, erosion of soil, etc. So experts are needed to make sure that the different species are

HOW DO SUNFLOWERS GET THEIR NAME?

The head of the sunflower is round and flat with bright yellow petals like the sun's rays. During the day it turns its face to follow the sun, making sure it gets the maximum amount of light. Hence the name sunflower.

The plant is used in various ways. Its leaves are used as fodder for animals, the seeds can be eaten raw or roasted, and are also harvested to make sunflower oil. The yellow flowers are used to make dye.

safeguarded, that diseases are treated and new trees planted. In many countries there is a government organization called a forestry commission which is responsible for all these things.

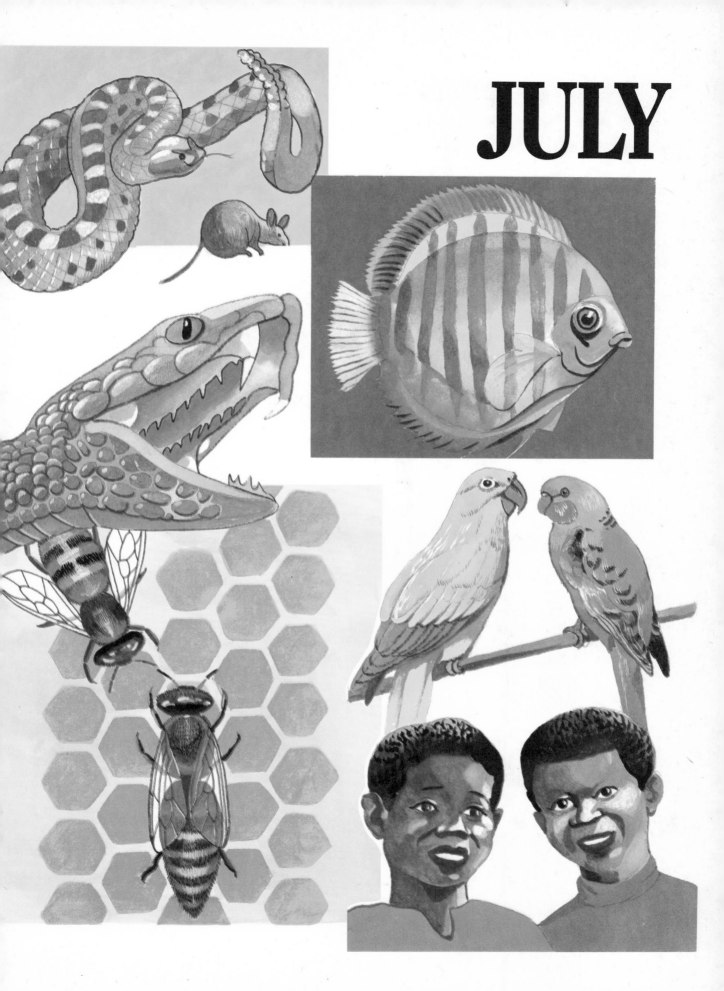

JULY

July 1

WHY DON'T ANIMALS SPEAK?

Animals communicate in all sorts of different ways; ravens caw and bees dance for example. Every species has some way of transmitting information to others of its kind. This is vital for feeding, mating and warning against danger or attack.

Human speech, which is symbolic and much more complicated than that of animals, transmits a great deal of varied information, and this requires a higher level of intelligence.

July 2

WHY DO SOME ANIMALS KILL OTHERS?

Animals don't usually kill for sport. If one animal kills another, it is usually for food, or in self-defense.

Meat-eating animals, or carnivores, kill vegetable-eating animals, or herbivores, to eat them, as they cannot digest vegetable matter themselves. A natural circle called the food chain is established which enables the different species to survive. Man can eat both meat and vegetables (an omnivore).

July 3

WHY ARE ANIMALS ABLE TO SWIM ALMOST AS SOON AS THEY ARE BORN?

All animals are born with the ability to swim or at least float in water. Their instinct makes them co-ordinate their movements so that they can float. However, this instinctive behavior has been replaced in humans by learned behavior, and it is the fear of sinking which makes us more likely to do so. We tend to move awkwardly in the water until we have learned to swim.

fabrics gradually developed, until nowadays most clothes are made from synthetic fibers. For certain things, like shoes or bags, leather continues to be the main raw material. However, some animal skins, particularly furs, are used because they are beautiful or rare, and they are a very expensive luxury.

July 4

WHY ARE SOME COATS AND BAGS MADE FROM ANIMAL SKINS?

Primitive man used the animal skins he obtained from hunting to protect himself against the cold. Later, the loom was invented, and the techniques of making

July 5

WHY DO SOME ANIMALS HIBERNATE ALL WINTER?

Cold-blooded animals need external heat for their bodies to stay active. In winter, when the temperature drops, they become sluggish and their body movements slow down a great deal, and so do their digestion and breathing. Tortoises are good examples of this.

Some warm-blooded animals, such as the bear, also become very sluggish and slow in winter due to the lack of food in the cold season. During the hibernation period a bear lives on the fat stored beneath the skin in various parts of its body.

July 6 — WHY DON'T ANIMALS WEAR CLOTHES?

The physical make-up of an animal's body is adapted to the environment in which it lives. Whales, for instance, have a thick layer of fat, and polar bears have very thick coats, and these enable both of them to withstand very low temperatures in their natural environment. Certain cold-blooded animals can adapt perfectly to changes in temperature.

Man has now spread throughout the world, and although his own body cannot adapt in the same way as an animal's, he has overcome the difficulty by using various technical means – and wearing an overcoat is one of them!

After he had learned to tame certain animals for transport, farming and food, he began to exploit other natural resources. Hunting stopped being a necessity and became a sport. Nowadays hunting is still a popular sport in all its forms, such as foxhunting, shooting and fishing.

July 7 — WHY DO PEOPLE HUNT ANIMALS?

Man has always needed animals in order to survive. Before he knew how to tame them, primitive man hunted them for their meat, skins, and bones.

July 8 — WHY DO SOME PEOPLE EAT ANIMALS?

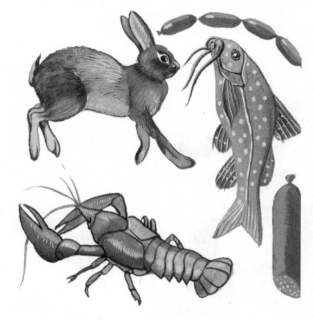

Man is an omnivore and so can eat both meat and vegetables. He could actually get all the nutrition he needs from vegetables alone – and some people do – but in general meat is eaten for two reasons. Most societies greatly enjoy the variety and flavor of meals that can be made with different meats. They also eat it because it is rich in the protein which is essential for a healthy body. However a carefully balanced vegetarian diet can also provide adequate proteins.

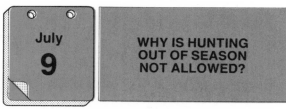

July
9

WHY IS HUNTING OUT OF SEASON NOT ALLOWED?

Modern guns are very refined, accurate, and swift. From a sporting point of view, this means that the hunter of wild animals has an unfair advantage. As a result, some species of animals are already extinct and others are threatened with extinction. Governments are therefore trying to prevent this from happening by forbidding hunting at certain times, particularly during the mating season.

July
10

WHY IS A DOG A MAN'S BEST FRIEND?

Dogs have this reputation all over the world, and indeed dogs have been domestic animals since very ancient times. The dog was man's companion during the Bronze Age, and has always been of great assistance in all kinds of tasks: as hunting dog, sheepdog and guard dog, for example, as well as being just a good friend. A dog is irreplaceable as a companion; his intelligence, reliability and friendly nature are well-known.

Obvious examples of these qualities are guide dogs who are trained to lead their blind masters, or the St Bernard dogs who, in the dangerous mountains of the Alps, go to the rescue of climbers who are injured or have lost their way.

July
11

WHY DO DOGS PANT?

All living beings need to get rid of excess heat for their metabolism (all the chemical processes that occur in the body) to work normally. Depending on the physical make-up of the species, this heat is lost in different ways. Humans and horses have sweat glands and pores in their skin: moisture comes out through the pores and evaporates, cooling the skin. Whales do this through the edges of their fins. Dogs, however, have very few pores or sweat glands, and have to get rid of the heat through their tongues. This is why they pant in hot weather or when they've been running around.

iris closes to protect the cells of the retina from being damaged by too much light. When the light is very dim, it expands to allow more in.

In cats and other felines, the iris is able to expand more than in other animals, to allow as much light as possible to enter, and so they are able to see perfectly well even when it seems dark to us.

July 12 — WHY ARE CATS ABLE TO SEE IN THE DARK?

The eyes of all higher animals contain a muscular structure called the iris, which works in the same way as the aperture of a camera. When the light is very bright, the

July 13 — WHY DO HORSES WEAR HORSESHOES?

During its evolution, the horse has lost four of its five original toes, and has ended up with one toe for each of its four limbs on which to support itself. Although this may seem a disadvantage, in fact, it makes the horse very well adapted for running,

cows, for example) have a different organic structure from other animals. Their stomachs are divided into four compartments, and when the animal grazes, the grass is swallowed almost whole and is deposited in the belly, the first of the stomachs. It undergoes a first digestion there, then it is returned to the mouth where it is chewed, and then it goes to the other three stomachs. It is quite common to find sheep lying on the ground and chewing in this manner, and this is known as chewing the cud.

because of the small area of contact with the ground.

The toenail is very highly developed, and is called the hoof. Although it is very tough, it wears away over a period of time, so man protects it with the horseshoe. Horseshoes are made of iron, are nailed on, and stop the hoof from wearing down.

July

14

WHY DO SHEEP ALWAYS SEEM TO BE CHEWING?

Nature has given this characteristic to animals such as sheep who, while they are grazing, are watched by carnivores such as wolves and eagles. Only when they are safe in their pens do they actually chew the food they have eaten.

All ruminating animals (sheep, goats and

July

15

WHY DO HENS LAY EGGS?

Hens are oviparous, or egg-laying animals. This means that they lay fertilized eggs, and the egg develops outside the mother; unlike viviparous animals such as mammals, in which the embryo grows inside the mother (as in humans). The egg, which contains the ovum and a large quantity of food reserves, is covered by a protective shell, and if the egg is fertilized, a baby chick will grow inside and eventually break this open.

However, once a fertilized egg is laid, it has to be kept warm for the chick to develop, which is why the hen sits on top of her eggs. This is called incubation.

July 16

WHY DO CAMELS HAVE HUMPS?

Everyone knows that the camel is the animal which is best adapted to traveling long distances in the desert, as it does not need to drink very often. It possesses this extraordinary quality thanks to its humps, which are fat stores. When the camel has to go without food or drink for a long time, it uses the fat from its humps to sustain itself.

July 17

WHY ARE SOME SNAKES POISONOUS?

Some snakes, particularly the smaller ones, are poisonous. They use the poison not only to defend themselves but to attack and paralyze their prey. Snakes have poison glands on either side of their heads, and tubes lead from them down into the hollow front teeth, or fangs, of the snake. When it bites, the poison is injected, and the effect of these snake poisons is swift and lethal, especially for small animals.

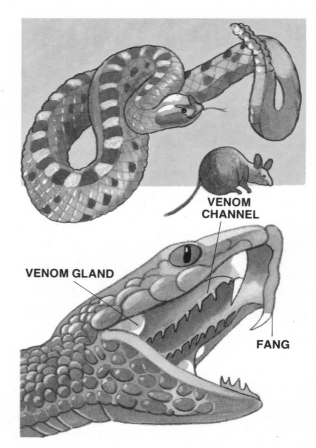

VENOM CHANNEL

VENOM GLAND

FANG

to rise into the air. Once in flight, it uses rising air currents to stay in the air without getting tired.

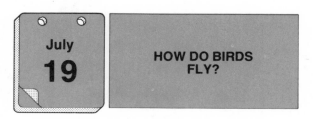

July 18 — WHY DO WE GET MILK FROM COWS?

All mammals need milk as a source of food during the early stages of life. Milk is rich in proteins, vitamins, and fat.

Cows' udders are very developed, and produce large quantities of milk. Because they are such gentle creatures, humans are able to milk them. Cows' milk is one of our major food sources.

July 20 — WHY DO FISH NEVER SEEM TO SLEEP?

Fish need to sleep to renew their energy just the same as other creatures. However, they always appear to have their eyes open as they have no eyelids. As sunlight loses part of its intensity when it passes through water, it cannot damage the retina of the fish – so they have no need for eyelids, and always look as if they are awake.

July 19 — HOW DO BIRDS FLY?

The pectoral muscles of birds, attached to their breastbones, are very strong and well-developed, and enable the bird to flap its wings very quickly. This forces air down under the wings, leaving a vacuum above which pulls the bird upwards and allows it

WHY DO DUCKS HAVE WEBBED FEET?

Ducks belong to the web-footed family of birds. All birds with webbed feet like the water, and during evolution the toes of these creatures have gradually been linked together by a skin, or web, which makes them well adapted to swimming. As the feet have a large surface area, they can paddle the bird along more swiftly in the water.

WHY DO WE PUT SCARECROWS IN FIELDS?

Birds feed mainly on insects and are very useful to man because they get rid of so many of these destructive creatures. However, they also like eating seeds and fruit, so farmers put stuffed figures which look like men into their fields and orchards to frighten the birds away.

In modern fields, acoustic birdscarers are used which reproduce the sounds of birds giving alarm cries, and so scare them away. There are also other birdscarers which make sounds like guns being fired.

WHY ARE PARROTS ABLE TO TALK?

Parrots can imitate the sound of the human voice because they have tongues which are similar to man's. Cockatoos and rooks have the same ability.

Of course, the sounds the birds make are not really like speaking as they are just imitating noises and not communicating information, and they usually have a very limited vocabulary. Human speech cannot be reproduced unless there is a higher level of intelligence.

An ants' colony can contain hundreds of thousands of ants, scattered along a series of intricate galleries. They need large quantities of food to feed so many insects, so the adults spend a great deal of time carrying seeds and other food to the nest to feed the developing larvae and younger insects, and to store food for the winter.

Ants' colonies are usually underground, and sometimes have chambers between the galleries. Food is stored in them, and certain ants are responsible for looking after the stores so that they don't go bad.

July 24 — **HOW CAN SOME FISH EXIST IN FREEZING WATERS?**

Fish are perhaps the most sensitive of all creatures to changes in their surroundings, such as temperature and saltiness. Nevertheless, different varieties are adapted to different conditions. Some fish can live only in tropical waters; others only in cold waters. And these fish, which like reptiles are cold-blooded animals, regulate their body temperature to suit the conditions, and slow down all activity to a minimum in the winter.

July 25 — **WHY ARE ANTS ALWAYS LOOKING FOR FOOD?**

July 26 — **WHY DO SPIDERS SPIN WEBS?**

A spider spins its web to capture the small insects on which it feeds. The threads of the web are made of a sticky substance from which the insects cannot escape. The spider is the only one who does not stick to it, but can walk on it without difficulty. Once the web is spun, the spider moves to the side to wait for its victims. When they are trapped, their struggles to escape produce vibrations on the web which alert the spider, and it jumps forward and paralyzes them.

July 27 — HOW DO FISH BREATHE IN WATER?

As fish live in water they have a breathing system quite unlike that of animals which live on land. By using their gills, they take oxygen from the water without needing to swallow it. The fish takes water in through its mouth and passes the water over the gills which are on either side of its head. These then filter out the oxygen which is dissolved in the water, and the rest of the water is expelled out behind the gills, which can open.

So that fish can breathe, the water they live in has to contain plenty of oxygen. So if you keep fish in a fish tank you should make sure the water contains enough oxygen for the type and number of fish in it, for instance by using an oxygenizer.

July 28 — WHY DO BEES PRODUCE HONEY?

There are three classes of bee in the bee world – queens, workers, and drones.

Worker bees make the honey, using nectar collected from flowers and special saliva produced by the bee. The honey is used to feed the developing larvae in the first stages of life and the adult bees during the winter months. Man has learned to take the honey to sweeten and flavor his food. Honey is an energy-giving food, rich in vitamins.

July 29 — WHY DO WE KILL FLIES WITH INSECTICIDES?

Flies live and breed in dirty, germ-ridden places like garbage dumps and carry these germs on their bodies. Man tries to kill them to stop them from spreading the germs of infection and dangerous diseases.

Spraying the flies with insecticides is one of the best ways of killing them. The sprays are unpleasant to humans, but deadly to insects, as they attack their breathing mechanism. All food should be covered when these sprays are being used.

to living things. They produce a great number of illnesses, some of them very serious, like typhoid, cholera, or rabies. This is why scientists are constantly researching ways of fighting these microorganisms.

July
31

WHY DO INSECT BITES SWELL?

When some insects bite they also inject an irritant liquid which is deadly for very small animals but has little effect on humans and other higher animals.

When an insect stings a human it usually produces a small swelling. This is the result of a reaction against the toxic liquid, and the bump is formed by a collection of dead, white blood cells.

July
30

WHY DO SCIENTISTS STUDY MICRO-ORGANISMS?

Although many microbes are very useful to man, such as those needed to make cheese, beer, and antibiotics, there are also plenty of others which are very dangerous

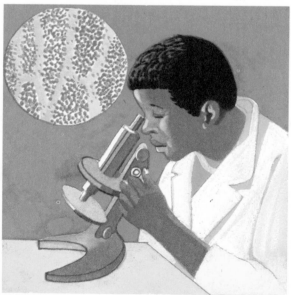

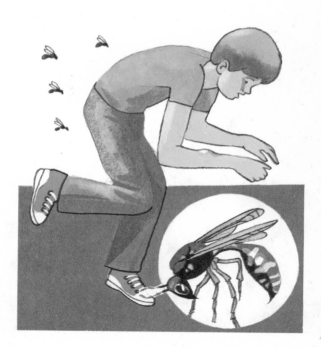

AUGUST

August 1

WHY ARE PEOPLE SCARED OF BATS?

These winged mammals, who sleep during the day and are active at night, have always had the reputation for being evil, even though most of them are really quite harmless.

But there is one American variety which does drink blood and attacks animals and men. This bat has well-developed incisor teeth which it uses to puncture the skin of the victim, and then it licks the blood which flows from the wound. The victim does not feel this.

Natives of South America, who are used to sleeping out in the open, have to wrap themselves up in their ponchos to protect themselves against attacks by these bats.

August 2

WHY ARE SOME HORSES CALLED THOROUGHBREDS?

The thoroughbred is a fairly recent creation, and it was the English who were the most determined to achieve this. The line is traced back to three horses from the Middle East, and only those horses who are directly descended from those three are considered to be true thoroughbreds. The thoroughbred is probably best known as a race horse and is bred mainly in Great Britain.

August 3

WHY DO TORTOISES LIVE SO LONG?

In general, the life span of animals in the wild is decided more by their ability to defend themselves against attack than by their physical make-up. This is why tortoises are particularly well adapted for survival, despite their slow movements. Their strong shells, into which they retreat when threatened with danger, make them able to withstand almost any attacker except man. So they are able to survive for a long time, and some species can even live to be 150 years old. Giant tortoises that weigh over 230 kilos (about 500 pounds) live in the remote Galapagos Islands.

As well as their real eyes, which are at the front of their heads, many butterflies have patterns which look like eyes on their wings. This is an excellent system of defense, because it confuses enemies who try to attack the butterfly.

Dolphins have always had a reputation for friendliness to man. Groups of dolphins often follow small ships and play about in the wake. More recently, the animal has been found to have several amazing qualities: a rare homing instinct, an unerring sense of direction and extraordinary powers of detection. Aquariums, where tame dolphins perform quite complicated tricks are very popular, and show how interested people are in this friendly mammal.

We know it happens, but we don't know why. Bird specialists have put forward all sorts of theories to do with instinct, astronomy, the sun, magnetism or geography to explain how they find their way back, but nobody really knows the

reason. In August every year swallows, obeying their migratory instinct, return in large flocks to the countries of Europe. There, they fly over the nesting areas and then each one returns to its own former nest.

August 7

WHY DOES AN ELEPHANT NEVER FORGET?

Although an elephant's brain is small in relation to the size of its body, it still has a brain with an extraordinary number of folds which give it a tremendous memory. So we say that someone who remembers things well has a memory like an elephant's.

August 8

HOW DOES THE ARCHER FISH CATCH ITS PREY?

The archer fish, which is very common in the Indian Ocean, has an unusual way of

catching insects. There is a groove in the roof of its mouth, and the fish can press on this with such force that the jet of water which shoots from its mouth stuns the insects. It can then catch and eat them.

August 9

WHY DOES THE CHAMELEON CHANGE COLOR?

For a long time people thought that this lizard changed the color of its skin as a form of defense, to hide by blending in with its surroundings. We now know this is not the real reason, although the chameleon does take advantage of this form of disguise. The color changes are really a result of the sun's rays on its skin, and the effects of its nerves when they are

stimulated by anger or fear. These make the color cells expand or contract, causing the changes in color for which the chameleon is so famous.

August 10

WHY ARE EELS CAUGHT AT NIGHT?

Elvers, or young eels, arrive on European coastlines in the thousands and swim up the rivers and estuaries into the marshes. As they tend to stay together in groups, fishermen can catch them in large quantities, but it has to be done at night with the help of a bright light. The eels are attracted by the light into the nets which the fishermen spread on the water, and so they are caught in batches.

August 11

WHY DO HERONS SLEEP STANDING ON ONE LEG?

Herons are water birds which feed on fish, shellfish, frogs, and toads. They have large, slender and featherless feet, and live mainly in marshes or shallow rivers. They

These magnificent birds possess beautiful multi-colored tails which open out in a large fan. They come originally from Southern India where they still live in the wild.

As is often the case among animals and birds, the male birds are much more brightly colored than the females. The males, or peacocks, spread their tails during the mating season to get the attention of the females, or peahens, who are attracted to the bright feathers of the male.

August
13

WHY ARE SALMON BECOMING MORE RARE?

also sleep there, standing on one leg, apparently to keep the other leg out of the cold. In this way the heron achieves the best balance of heat exchange between its body and the water while it is resting.

August
12

WHY DO PEACOCKS DISPLAY THEIR FEATHERS?

Salmon, a great delicacy, were once plentiful, but now they are threatened with extinction. There are two main reasons for this: increasing pollution in rivers, which kills many fish, and the alteration of the natural course of rivers when man builds hydroelectric dams. In order to spawn (lay their eggs), salmon need to swim up rivers to reach pure, running streams containing plenty of oxygen; the dams prevent them doing this. Modern fish farmers, who want to preserve this species, have had to reserve and create special breeding zones where salmon are able to find perfect conditions for laying their eggs.

front legs. The short front legs are used for holding and feeding, and the back legs are long and powerful. Its tail is also strong and muscular, and with a push from its tail, the kangaroo can spin round suddenly on its back legs and leap forward as much as 9 meters (29 feet).

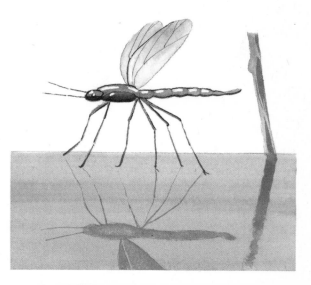

August
14

HOW DO KANGAROOS JUMP?

Although it is a four-legged animal, this creature of the Australian outback has back legs which are very much longer than its

August
15

HOW DO POND SKATERS FLOAT?

These insects have a large slender body with thin legs which they can make longer or shorter, and which are coated with an oily substance that is resistant to water. The surface tension of the water acts as a supporting skin on which the pond skaters can float. They can also skim rapidly across the water like water skiers. Some pond skaters are wingless but others can fly.

August
16

WHY DO BIRDS MIGRATE?

In the winter, nature seems to come to a standstill. There is no fruit and hardly any insects; worms and frogs become slow and

The long-legged ostrich is the largest living bird. Although it cannot fly, it can run faster than a horse, and has some strange habits and unexpected reactions. It usually eats insects, fruit, and seeds, but it has been known to eat the most unlikely things, such as stones, shells, wood, or even metal objects. It will usually run away from its enemies though if it is cornered, it can kick powerfully. Otherwise, when faced with danger, it stands in a clumsy, frightened way, hiding its head under its wing.

sleepy and small molluscs bury themselves in the mud. Birds discover that their natural sources of food have disappeared, so they have to fly to climates where they can find food more easily. Later, when the climate becomes warmer again, they will return home.

| August 17 | WHY DOES AN OSTRICH HIDE ITS HEAD UNDER ITS WING? |

| August 18 | WHY DO SNAKES SHED THEIR SKINS? |

Not all naturalists agree on this, but most think that the reason snakes shed their skins several times a year is that as the snake gradually grows, the outer skin becomes too tight. Eventually it comes off like a dry husk or shell, allowing the new skin underneath to emerge.

August 19 — WHERE DO TAILOR BIRDS GET THEIR NAME?

Birds build their nests in many unusual ways. But perhaps the most surprising of all is the nest of the tailor bird, which is clothed on the outside with wide leaves delicately sewn together with strong vegetable fibers. It uses its thin, pointed beak like a needle, punching holes in the leaves, and pulling the "thread" through.

August 20 — WHY ARE PIRANHA FISH DANGEROUS?

Although they are usually small — not more than 25 centimeters (8 inches) long — piranha fish are some of the fiercest predators of rivers and seas. They live in tropical waters such as the Amazon and Orinoco Basins, and their mouths are full of sharp, pointed teeth. They swim in large numbers which make them terrible enemies, as a shoal of piranha fish can devour much larger creatures in a few minutes.

August 21 — WHAT MAKES THE PRAYING MANTIS SO INTERESTING?

117

This slender, delicately colored grasshopper, found in warm or tropical regions, is famous for three unusual characteristics. Its neck is amazingly mobile; it is able to bend and lift its front legs together as if in prayer; and the female often kills her mate when mating has finished.

August

22

WHY IS IT HARD FOR THE ALBATROSS TO TAKE OFF?

Albatrosses live by catching fish in the seas around Australia. They are very large birds, and have a wingspan which is often greater than 3 meters (9 feet). They are very friendly, and like to follow and glide above ships in the open sea. However, because

they only ever land on the ground to build their nests, they cannot take off very well, and, like airplanes, they need plenty of room for take-off.

August

23

HOW DOES AN ELECTRIC RAY FIGHT ITS ENEMIES?

The electric ray (torpedo fish) is flat with a plate-shaped back, and a tail. It has an unusual weapon in the form of two large electrical organs in the body and the pectoral fins. Any predator trying to attack the ray is driven off by a powerful discharge of as much as 200 volts or 2,000 watts – enough to light up 33 electric light bulbs. It catches its own prey by stunning them with a shock.

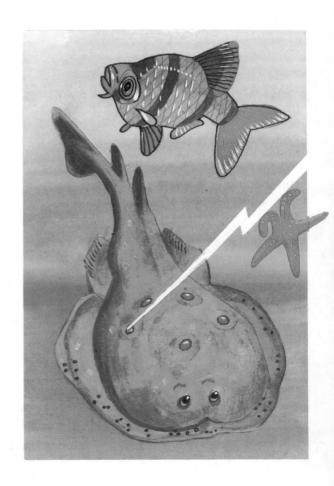

<table>
<tr>
<td>

August
24

</td>
<td>

WHY DO CRICKETS SING?

</td>
</tr>
</table>

Actually, crickets don't sing — they use their bodies like instruments to produce the sound. Have you ever heard the happy ''chirp chirp'' of crickets in the country? Male crickets make this sound when their front wings are at an angle of 45° and they rub them together. A scraper on one forewing rubs against many little ''teeth'' on the other forewing, and this produces the song.

<table>
<tr>
<td>

August
25

</td>
<td>

WHY DON'T PEOPLE CATCH COLDS IN THE ANTARCTIC?

</td>
</tr>
</table>

The South Pole is colder than the North Pole, and the temperature often falls to −80°C. No microorganisms can survive at such low temperatures; even viruses resistant to extreme temperatures like the common cold cannot survive there.

<table>
<tr>
<td>

August
26

</td>
<td>

WHY IS THE CAPERCAILLIE DIFFICULT TO CAPTURE?

</td>
</tr>
</table>

The capercaillie, a plump species of European grouse with bright, colorful plumage, is extremely timid and likes to live in lonely places which are very awkward to reach. In order to catch it, hunters have to wait for the mating season, when the bird's

119

shyness disappears and it behaves quite differently. It does a kind of mad dance, weaving its feet in and out if it's perched on a tree branch, or strutting about on the ground, proudly displaying its feathers to attract a female bird. This gives the hunter his opportunity to capture it.

August
27

HOW DO OWLS KEEP SO STILL?

The owl, a common visitor to church belfries and old ruined towers, is a night bird which sits very still for long periods of time. It has very sharp hearing, but because its eyes are at the front of its head its vision is not very well developed. However, since it can turn its head almost right around it can keep a constant lookout without altering its position. Because it is able to do this, and because of the long, drawn out piercing shriek it makes, this bird of prey is not very popular.

August
28

WHY DO SOME REPTILES HAVE THREE EYES?

It seems incredible, but there really are reptiles that have a third eye on the upper part of their head. Nowadays, because this eye is not used it cannot see. It corresponds, to the pineal gland in other living beings, including man. Scientists have not yet discovered what the function of this gland is.

August
29

HOW DOES BIRD'S NEST SOUP GET ITS NAME?

There is a type of swift in the far south of Asia which makes the outside of its nest using a special saliva. This saliva forms a coating when it comes into contact with the air, but dissolves easily in water. The outside part of the nests are highly prized in oriental cookery. A tasty soup is made from them, which is known all over the world as bird's nest soup.

This clever rodent possesses a beautiful and valuable skin. It is an amphibian which lives in freshwater rivers and on the edges of lakes. There is no animal that can match it for hard work and skill, and the care it takes in building river dams.

The beaver gnaws at the foot of great tree trunks to fell the trees; it then skilfully places them in the river to trap its prey. It strengthens the dam with clay which it collects with its broad tail, to produce a structure an engineer would be proud of.

Sadly, the number of beavers has been greatly reduced by men hunting them for their skins, and now they are a protected species in several countries.

August 30
WHY IS THE BEAVER A PROTECTED SPECIES?

August 31
WHY IS IT AGAINST THE LAW TO HUNT CERTAIN BIRDS OF PREY?

Vultures and other large birds of prey carry out a very necessary job. Without them, the decaying dead bodies of animals would create serious health risks, particularly in hot countries. Many of these species are therefore protected by special laws in most countries. In addition, they are becoming extinct as a result of uncontrolled hunting.

SEPTEMBER

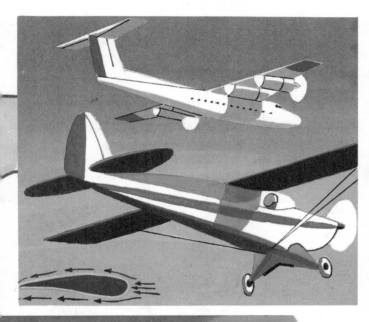

September 1

WHY DO YOU PUT WATER IN CAR RADIATORS?

When gas is burned in a car engine it gives off a lot of heat, which affects the various parts of the engine. Although the heat only rises slowly it could cause the engine to seize up. So these parts have to be cooled by water which circulates around the engine in special channels.

The water first passes through the radiator which is made up of lots of thin pipes, kept cool by the air which blows against them as the vehicle is moving. The cooling action is also helped by a fan turned by the engine. This water is carried around the rest of the engine to cool it down. Heat is transferred to the water which returns to the radiator and is cooled again.

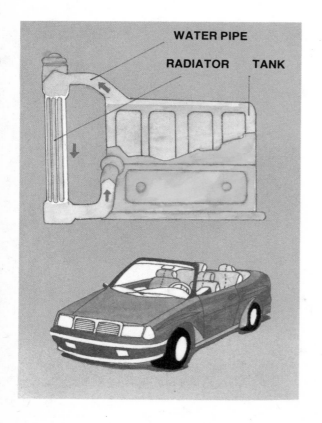

WATER PIPE

RADIATOR   TANK

September 2

WHY CAN'T ANIMALS BUILD MACHINES?

Man has a larger brain than any other animal. He can remember and understand large amounts of information, and has developed languages to pass on what he has learned. This high intelligence, and the way he can hold and manipulate tools, has enabled civilized man to make machines. Although some of the more intelligent animals like chimpanzees are able to use basic machines, only man knows how to invent and build them.

September 3

WHY DO CARS STOP WHEN THEY RUN OUT OF GAS?

All engines require some source of energy to make them work. Gas is a type of fuel which releases a large amount of stored energy when burned: the modern car uses gas.

Inside the car engine a mixture of gas and air is burned. This causes a series of small explosions which push the pistons up and down, and make the engine work. Without gas there would be no explosions, no energy, and the car could not move.

Vehicles nowadays have a gauge which shows how much fuel there is in the tank. It often saves the driver running out of gas.

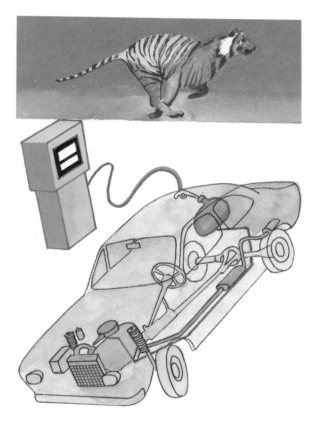

warmer the air, the higher it will rise into the sky.

The first hot air balloons were used in 1783, and they are still used today for sport, advertising, and weather research.

Airships and other sorts of closed balloons are filled with helium. This gas is lighter than air, and non-inflammable, but very expensive.

September
5

WHY DO CARS HAVE SEVERAL GEARS?

The gears in a car are connected with the engine, and decide how hard the engine

September
4

HOW DO HOT AIR BALLOONS FLY?

Hot air balloons use the scientific principle that hot air always rises. To take off, the pilot casts off the ballast (heavy bags) which act as an anchor, and sends a jet of flame into the inflated balloon. The

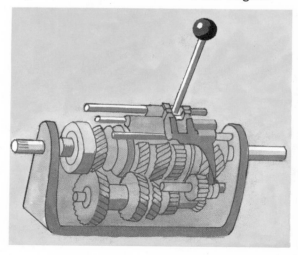

works. When a car first starts moving the engine has to work very hard, and usually sounds noisy. This is when the driver uses the first gear. He can soon change up to second gear by pressing the clutch and moving the gear lever; then third, and finally fourth and sometimes fifth. The car will now be moving fast and quietly, as the car's weight traveling on a flat or downhill road helps it move along without much work from the engine.

If the car has to go uphill, the driver will have to change down to third or even second gear to get the extra power needed. The reverse gear enables the car to go backwards. Gears in a car have the same function as the gears on a bicycle.

September 6

HOW DO AIRPLANES FLY WHEN THEY ARE SO HEAVY?

The flying mechanism of an airplane is quite different from that of a bird. There are two main reasons why it flies. The powerful engines push it forward with an enormous thrust of energy, and the design of the wings creates greater pressure under the aircraft than above it when it moves forward. This low pressure sucks the airplane up into it, so we can say that they fly suspended in the area of low pressure they produce above their wings.

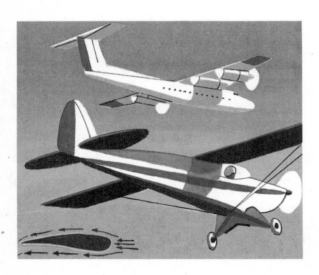

September 7

WHY DO CARS NEED OIL?

A car engine is made up of many moving parts which touch each other. This constant movement of metal together causes friction (rubbing) and creates unwanted heat. Oil is good for lubricating machinery (making it smooth and slippery), and is used in car engines to reduce the friction. As some of the oil burns away with the heat, and some leaks out of the system, it has to be replaced from time to time.

September 8

WHY DO AIRPLANES SOMETIMES BREAK THE SOUND BARRIER?

Thanks to their powerful engines, jet airplanes can travel at extremely high speeds. Sound is transmitted in the form of waves, which travel very fast and always at the same speed. If an object such as an

airplane flies by keeping its wings suspended in the vacuum it creates for itself in the air, so if that air becomes too scarce, as it does outside the earth's atmosphere, it cannot stay up. Also, the body of an aircraft is not designed to protect passengers from the lack of atmospheric pressure. So even the most modern aircraft rarely go more than 15 kilometers (9 miles) above the ground.

September 10

HOW CAN HELICOPTERS HOVER IN THE AIR IN ONE SPOT?

The shape of the blades on top of a helicopter, and the speed with which they rotate, makes them produce a very strong air current beneath them. This pulls the helicopter upwards and keeps it in the air. It can stay in one spot, rise, fall, or move forward, according to the way it is controlled.

airplane goes as fast as, or faster than sound, the sound waves made by the engine noise produce a shock wave which makes a great bang, and this is called breaking the sound barrier.

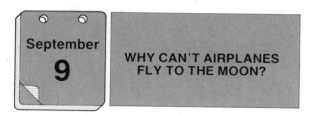

September 9

WHY CAN'T AIRPLANES FLY TO THE MOON?

Firstly, airplanes cannot fly fast enough to escape the pull of gravity. Next, an

HOW DO ARTIFICIAL SATELLITES STAY IN SPACE?

Powerful rockets carry artificial satellites beyond the atmosphere. Once they are in space, the rocket gives the satellite a great thrust of speed and sends it on its permanent journey. The satellite is subject to two forces – that supplied by the rocket which keeps it moving, and the pull of the earth's gravity which keeps it from traveling further away into space – and these keep it in orbit around the earth. Satellites are used for transmitting scientific information back to Earth, and for communication across the world.

September
12

HOW ARE SHIPS WEIGHING MANY TONS ABLE TO FLOAT?

Ships stay afloat in spite of their great weight because they are hollow. For this reason they have a density which is less than that of water, and the total weight of the ship is less than the weight of the water that has been displaced. This produces pressure against the bottom of the ship which keeps it afloat.

September
13

HOW DO SCUBA DIVERS BREATHE UNDERWATER?

Men cannot breathe underwater like fish, because their breathing system is not capable of obtaining oxygen directly from the water. Instead, a scuba diver carries bottles filled with compressed air which he wears attached to his back. When he is underwater he can breathe the air from the bottles through a mouthpiece which is connected to them by special rubber tubes.

September
14

HOW DOES RADAR DETECT OBJECTS WHEN IT IS DARK?

Radar is a method used for detecting the presence and speed of moving objects which are a long way away. It is also useful at night.

A radar transmitter sends out a series of short radio waves, and when they meet an object, it reflects the waves back to the transmitter as an echo. The transmitter picks these up, records them, and can work out the position and speed of the object from the direction of the waves and the time they take to be reflected. This position is then shown on a special screen. Radar can therefore detect objects both in the daytime and at night, as it does not need light.

September **15** | HOW DO WE SEE THINGS ON TELEVISION?

In a television studio a camera captures images and they are changed into waves which are transmitted into the air. The aerials of the television sets in people's houses pick these waves up and immediately change them into a series of colored dots in the television tube inside their set. This is behind the screen, and so shows on it a picture which is identical to the one being transmitted. This complicated process takes only a very short time, so the television can show a picture of something that is happening at the same moment somewhere else.

September **16** | WHY DO SOME PLUGS SPARK WHEN DISCONNECTED?

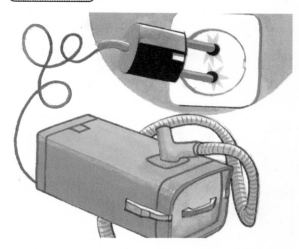

The electricity supplied to a building travels round a circuit in cables under the floor, and back to the main supply point. A plug socket is a point where there is a deliberate break or gap in that circuit. When you plug something in, the circuit is complete, and the electric current passes through the apparatus, making it work.

If you pull the plug out when the current is switched on, the contact surface of the plug pins gets smaller as it is pulled out. The ends of the pins heat up very quickly and then the remaining electricity in them jumps across the gap between the pins, which we see as a spark. You should always switch off an appliance before disconnecting it.

129

September 17 — HOW DO TELEPHONES WORK?

The way that telephones work is similar in some ways to television, but the transmission uses an electric current rather than air waves, and telephones transmit only sound, not pictures.

When you speak on the telephone, the microphone inside the mouthpiece transforms the sound waves into electrical impulses. These are transmitted through the telephone cable to the earpiece of the other person's receiver. This turns the impulses into sounds which are nearly identical to those made by the caller, so that it is like listening to the actual voice of the person talking.

Years ago, and still today in some isolated places, you had to ask the operator to connect your telephone with someone else's in order to speak to them. Today, thanks to the progress of electronics, the connection is made automatically, even to countries on the other side of the world.

September 18 — WHY DO ROADS SLOPE DOWN AT THE SIDES?

No doubt it would be much easier for car drivers if the roads were completely flat. It wouldn't be necessary to keep turning the steering wheel to stop the car from veering towards the edge of the road. The reason roads are made with a slight slope on either side is to carry rainwater away from the road surface. If this were flat, the rain would stay there, creating a nuisance and a danger to road users. The sloping edges encourage the water to flow away into the ditch or gutter and then to the drains.

September 19 — WHY DO WE SEE A REFLECTION IN A MIRROR?

Mirrors are made of polished metal, or glass which is coated on the back with a metal film such as silver or tin. These surfaces can reflect light almost completely without changing it. When we stand in front of a mirror, the light rays reflected by the body reach the surface of the mirror and are reflected back again towards us.

As it is a reflected image, it seems to be the other way round. Consequently, if the right hand is moved in front of the mirror, it looks as if the reflected image is moving its left hand. And if some writing is held up to the mirror, it is reflected back to front, making it difficult to read.

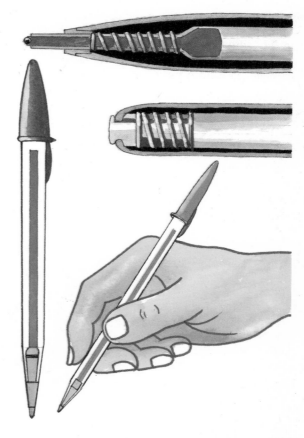

September 20

HOW DO BALLPOINT PENS GET THEIR NAME?

A ballpoint pen has several different parts. Inside the body of the pen is a long tube which is filled with a very thick ink, and which is joined to the point of the pen. There is a hole at the tip, which is closed by a small ball which revolves when we move it across paper, leaving behind it a trail of ink which is evenly spread. This is how the pen writes, and the small ball gives the pen its name.

September 21

HOW DOES A CAMERA TAKE PICTURES?

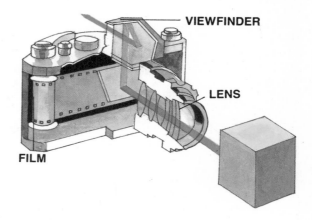

VIEWFINDER

LENS

FILM

131

The process itself is quite simple. Inside the camera, kept in complete darkness, is a roll of film coated with chemicals which react and change in the presence of light. When we take a picture of something, we press the camera button and a tiny window known as the shutter opens for a very short time. It allows the light to be reflected from the view on to a section of the film. The chemical substances react, creating patches in the surface of the film which correspond to this reflected light. The film is then developed, and printed onto paper which gives us a photograph.

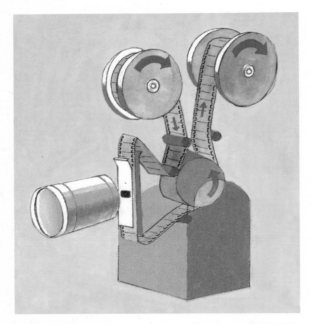

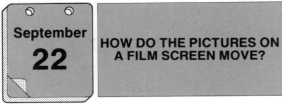

September
22
HOW DO THE PICTURES ON A FILM SCREEN MOVE?

The pictures don't really move, in fact, as a film is made up of many single shots, or stills. But the spectator thinks that they are moving because the retina in the eye, which transmits the images to the brain, does not wipe out the last image immediately. When the images are shown very quickly one after another, it creates the impression of movement.

Early silent films look jerky because they were filmed at 16 frames per second. Today they are shot at 24 frames per second.

September
23
HOW DOES A FLASHLIGHT PRODUCE A STRONG BEAM OF LIGHT?

A flashlight can produce a powerful light without being plugged into an electric current because it contains a small electric generator or battery. The battery contains two chemical substances which react together and produce energy when they are linked by an electric current. When the flashlight is switched on, the electrical current is complete, and the energy produced in the battery is used to make the beam of light. As the substances are gradually used up, the battery loses its power, and has to be replaced. Some batteries can be recharged by means of electricity.

WHY DO PEOPLE LOOK SO BIG ON A FILM SCREEN?

When we pass light through a film on to a screen a little distance away, we obtain a picture which is larger than the film itself. This is because there is a magnifying lens at the end of the projector. The size of the image depends on the distance between the projector and the screen, and on the focusing power at the end of the projector. Projectors also have a system of lenses which help to make the picture clearer and sharper.

tower, or other tall building, it will attract lightning towards it and carry the energy to the ground, where it is discharged without causing any harm. These are called lightning conductors.

Lightning occurs because the ground has a negative electric charge, while clouds have a positive electric charge. During certain weather conditions these charges increase and produce huge sparks, which are the flashes we see.

WHY DO TALL BUILDINGS HAVE LIGHTNING CONDUCTORS?

The energy and strength of a flash of lightning is enormous and can cause terrible destruction. Disasters can be avoided by making use of the fact that lightning will nearly always travel to the highest point of something that will conduct the electric charge to earth. If an electric conductor or cable is placed high up on a

WHY DO MAGNETS ATTRACT METAL OBJECTS?

Certain metals, and substances containing metal, change when they are subjected to a magnetic field, and this generates magnetism. The change is to do with the crystal structure of the metals, and with the electric charge which causes the magnetic field. The magnetism travels from one end of the magnet to the other.

Magnets are called "transitory" if they

are only magnetic while they are stimulated by a magnetic force. Other magnets are permanent, because they continue to be magnetic even when the stimulus from the magnetic object is no longer there.

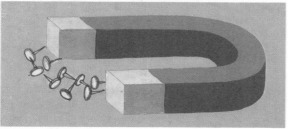

September
27

HOW IS MUSIC PUT ON A RECORD?

A record is a thin plastic disc upon which sound is recorded. Each side has a spiral groove, and the walls of the grooves go in and out. During recording, the sound is transmitted through a microphone to the instrument which cuts the walls of the grooves to different depths according to the changes in sound.

We use a record player to listen to the record, and this reverses the recording process. The grooves of the record make the needle of the record player vibrate, and these vibrations are made louder by an amplifier to reproduce the sound that was recorded.

September
28

HOW DOES A MATCH LIGHT?

The colored knob on the top of a matchstick is the head, which is usually made up of phosphorous and other substances. Phosphorous catches fire easily at a temperature of 50°C. When a match is struck on the rough side of the matchbox, the friction causes the head of the match to become very hot. The phosphorous catches fire and lights the wood or cardboard of the matchstick.

Because they ignite only when struck on the matchbox provided and not on other rough surfaces, they are known as safety matches.

exerted as this spring unwinds pushes a series of cogs and levers in a regular movement. The rhythmic motion produces the well-known "tick tock."

Modern electric or battery clocks don't tick because they do not have this mechanism.

September
30

HOW DO ESCALATORS WORK?

An escalator is a moving staircase which is made of stairs fixed to an electric conveyor belt. A system of levers operates the steps to form the staircase, and it is kept moving constantly either upward or downward. Some escalators are controlled by a photoelectric cell, so that they only work when someone is actually coming up or going down.

September
29

WHY DO SOME CLOCKS TICK?

Traditional clocks and watches work by means of a complicated mechanism. The clock has to be wound up to make it work. A spring inside tightens, and the force

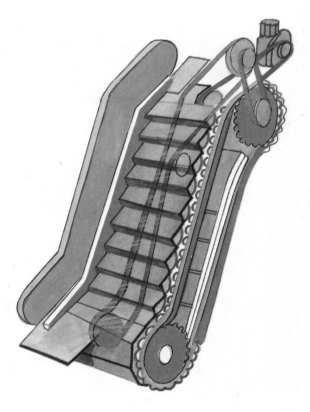

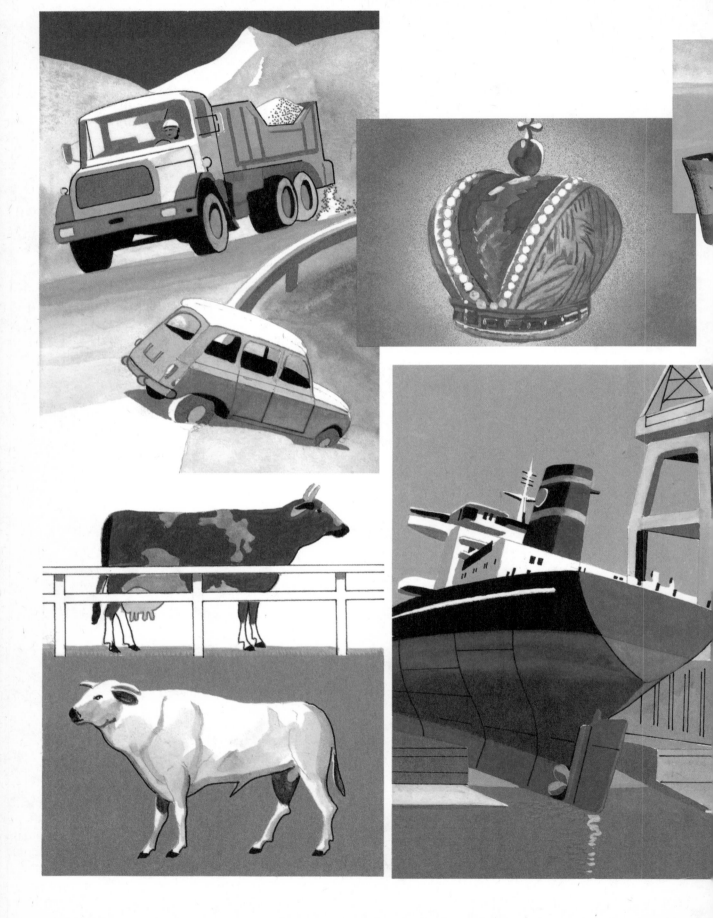

OCTOBER

October

1

HOW DOES A PERISCOPE WORK?

The first periscopes were invented in the middle of the last century. Their function is to enable people to see what is happening outside a vehicle or room without windows. They are mostly used in submarines when they are underwater or by army tanks.

A periscope consists of a long tube which can be raised or lowered, and can turn to face any direction. Inside there is a series of lenses with a prism (a triangular lens) at each end. The upper one reflects the view it can see vertically down to the lower one, which reflects it horizontally into the eye of the observer, and so by rotating the periscope, he has an all-round view of what is above him.

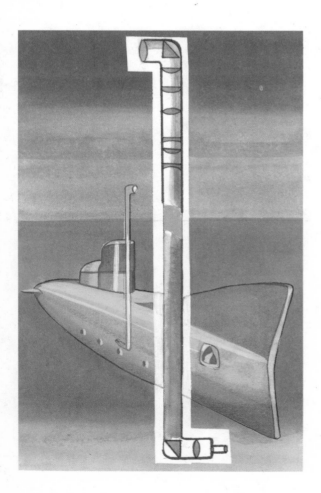

October

2

WHY WERE BRIDGES IN ANCIENT TIMES BUILT WITH ARCHES?

This building technique, often used by the Romans, began when it was discovered that an arch shape strengthens bridges, by distributing the weight of the bridge evenly on to the side supports. A famous example is the Roman bridge at Merida in western Spain: this bridge is 692 meters (756 yards) long, nearly 7 meters (7 yards) wide and originally it had 81 arches, though some were destroyed in 1812. The bridge is still open to traffic.

October

3

WHY DO LIQUIDS STAY HOT IN A THERMOS?

Inside a thermos there is a bottle which has a double wall of shiny glass. Between the two walls there is a vacuum. The heat or cold cannot escape through the vacuum, as it would through the sides of an ordinary jug. This bottle is in turn protected by a

some essential foods were not available. Today we preserve food by deep freezing, vacuum drying and canning.

The tin which is used to coat the inside of cans is a metal which can be used in contact with food. It is not poisonous, and does not rust, or corrode easily. Once food is sealed inside a sterilized can it will keep almost indefinitely without going bad, although some fruit acids will corrode the tin in time. It is very useful for campers and explorers who have no refrigerator.

October 5

WHAT MAKES SMOKE GO UP A CHIMNEY?

There is a basic law of physics called convection, which states that hot air always rises. Chimneys are tall and narrow to help convection to happen quickly. The fire at the bottom of the chimney produces heat. The heat rises, pulling the smoke up the chimney with it. This draws in air and fresh oxygen beneath the fire, which helps the fire burn well. Before houses had chimneys, the living spaces were very smoky.

metal or plastic coating, and is fixed into the container of the flask using rubber or any other material which will not conduct the heat. So when a hot – or cold – liquid is put into a flask and the top is sealed, it will stay at the same temperature for hours.

October 4

WHY ARE SOME FOODS CANNED?

People have always preserved food by drying, salting, or smoking it, so that they had enough to eat during the winter when

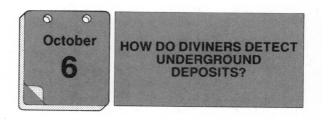

October 6

HOW DO DIVINERS DETECT UNDERGROUND DEPOSITS?

The practice of divining, using a forked hazel twig or a pendulum, which is said to move when it is held above deposits of metal or sources of water, was disliked by the Church and people in authority. It was believed the diviners were using evil powers.

Today, although we still cannot fully explain the reasons why it works, divining is carried out by many specialists to discover underground water and minerals. But the results are still the subject of much discussion.

October 7

WHY DO BOATS HAVE KEELS?

The keel which projects downward into the water is the main balancing part of a boat. If ships did not have keels, they would be very unstable, and there would be a constant danger of overturning because of rough waves or uneven loading of the cargo.

Each ship or boat has a differently shaped keel depending on its structure. In

general, sailing boats need deeper keels because their movements from side to side are more swift and sudden, while ordinary cargo ships have longer keels.

October 8

WHY ARE TELEVISION AERIALS HORIZONTAL?

All aerials are for picking up the waves sent into the air by a transmitter. For television they are transmitted horizontally, so the TV aerials hold the different tubes, which pick up the various channels, in a horizontal position, to gain the best reception.

October 9

WHY ARE SOME BOTTLE CORKS HELD ON WITH WIRE?

Champagne and other sparkling drinks are bottled before they have finished fermenting. The process continues in the bottle, and produces carbon dioxide gas which naturally creates pressure in the bottle. The neck of the bottle is designed to resist this, but not the cork. So when the restraining wire is removed, the cork pops out easily, forced out by the sparkling liquid.

October 10

WHY SHOULD UNTREATED MILK BE BOILED?

Milk, which is rich in fats, proteins and vitamins, is a complete food, but it is

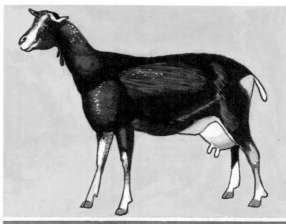

dangerous to drink it straight from the cow or goat. Untreated milk is a perfect breeding ground for bacteria, which if present can multiply very quickly. This is why it is best to boil the milk first to destroy any harmful microorganisms. Fresh milk will only keep if it is pasteurized and then only just for a few days, in a fridge, or if it is sterilized. Only treated milk is sold in shops.

October 11

HOW DID THE POSTAL SERVICE BEGIN?

Many years ago, when transport was limited to horseback and horsedrawn carriages, countries had a system of "staging posts." Travelers and messages were relayed from one to the next of these, using stagecoaches. Some of these postal messengers had to cover 160 kilometers (100 miles) per day on horseback, across vast territories.

little model figure of a monk with a movable hood, with a cord attached to it. When the air is dry, the cord twists, and when damp, it untwists, making the hood go up and down. Some countries have glass figures with a coating that changes color when the air is damp, or pine cones which open when it is damp and close when it is dry.

October 13

WHY ARE SOME PEARLS CALLED CULTURED PEARLS?

October 12

WHAT IS A HYGROSCOPE?

This is a device used to measure how damp the air is. Spanish households have a

Pearls are formed by oysters within their shells. A grain of sand gets inside the oyster and causes an irritation. The oyster then covers the sand with mother-of-pearl so that it becomes smooth and round. But for some years now, pearls have been obtained by artificially introducing tiny pieces of mother-of-pearl from other shells into the oysters. This stimulates them to produce pearls as good as the natural ones.

October 14
WHY DO WE KEEP FOOD IN A REFRIGERATOR?

Food goes bad because bacteria, mold and microbes attack it. This happens more quickly in warm temperatures, whereas cold interrupts and even stops this process. So food will keep fresh for longer in a refrigerator.

Nowadays, there are enormous refrigerated rooms for storing meat and vegetables which can then be eaten in perfectly good condition at any time of year. The technique of keeping foods refrigerated is most important in transporting fish from the sea to the markets where they are sold.

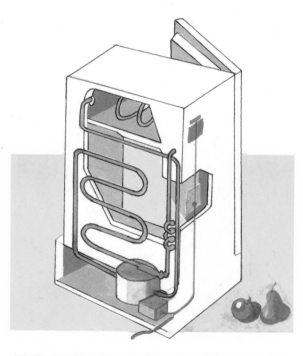

October 15
WHY IS ARTIFICIAL INSEMINATION USED?

This very widespread practice is used to breed the best and purest animal livestock. The hereditary characteristics are present

in the genes of the reproductive cells. Cows, for example, can be artificially inseminated from a bull of good stock, and produce calves of the same good stock, without ever seeing the bull. This process is also used successfully in the breeding of some fish, and in experimental research into plant behavior.

October 16
WHY DO PARACHUTES OPEN?

This clever invention was originally the idea of Leonardo da Vinci, but the Montgolfier brothers first put it into practice in 1779. Modern parachutes allow people to jump from airplanes and land safely on the ground.

There are parachutes for military, sporting, or exhibition uses, but they are all basically the same. The parachutist jumps and the ripcord is then pulled either by himself or automatically. The pilot parachute comes out of the backpack pulling the main canopy after it. The weight of the parachutist as he falls forces air into the

canopy, which opens like an umbrella. There is a hole on the surface of the canopy to act as a valve, controlling the fall.

October 17

HOW DO FILM CAMERAS "ZOOM IN?"

"Zooming in" is how a cameraman moves from a distant to a close-up shot when he is filming. It seems as if the camera is moving towards an object. Really the camera stays where it is, and the zoom

lens attached to the front of the camera is automatically adjusting its focus through a series of movable lenses.

October 18

WHY MUST DETERGENTS BE BIODEGRADABLE?

Detergents, which are chemical cleaning substances, are now used in homes, factories, and other institutions. Until recently, the waste products of most of them could not be dissolved. They were released into rivers and seas world-wide, where they floated and built up so much that this pollution was a serious threat to survival for many animals and plants. Health authorities recommend that detergents are made biodegradable, which means they break down naturally by biological action and no longer cause pollution.

October 19

HOW DOES A SUBMARINE DIVE?

The submarine body has a double outside wall, and in the space between

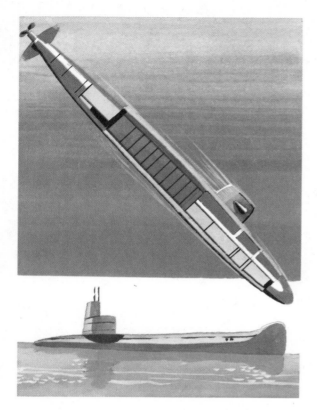

these two there are tanks which contain water or air, depending on whether the submarine is to submerge (dive) or emerge (surface). When submerging, valves let water in up to the desired level; when emerging, water is pumped out by appliances filled with compressed air which takes the place of the water. The more water pumped into the tanks, the deeper the submarine dives.

October 20 — WHY DO SOME DOORS OPEN BY THEMSELVES?

There are two mechanisms which operate an automatic door. One works when pedestrians step on a spring hidden in the floor approaching the doors; the other works when they are standing in the doorway and the doors cannot close safely. The pedestrian's body obstructs a beam of light from a photoelectric cell hidden in each of the two walls in front of the doors.

These doors will stay open until there is nothing in the way.

October 21 — WHY ARE METEOROLOGICAL SATELLITES IMPORTANT?

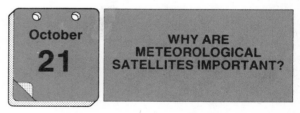

These inventions, pioneered by Sputnik 1, launched into space by the Soviet Union on 4th October 1957, have revolutionized the way weather is forecast. With satellites, which are in reality scientific laboratories in orbit around the earth, it is possible to photograph clouds and hurricanes as well

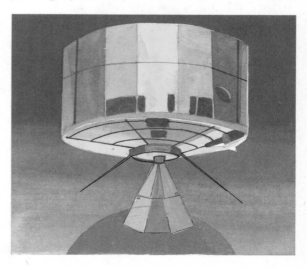

as icebergs, sand storms, and even monsoons. Many activities rely on the state of the weather – air and naval navigation, farming, radio and telephone communications have benefitted greatly. It is also possible to warn communities when a hurricane is heading straight for them, so that they can be taken to safety.

October 22

WHY IS SALT SPRINKLED ON ROADS WHEN IT SNOWS?

When snow comes into contact with salt it does not freeze. If snow is expected, or just fallen, trucks go out to spread a mixture of grit and salt on the roads. This stops the snow from turning to ice, which would make the roads dangerous for vehicles and pedestrians.

LIGHTHOUSE AT PHAROS, EGYPT

October 23

WHY DO WE HAVE LIGHTHOUSES ON THE COAST?

Lighthouses are designed to warn ships, by means of a flashing beam of light, that they are near a coastline. Long ago, bonfires were lit as warning signals along the coast to stop ships from being wrecked on the rocks. Later, towers were built. For example, in 280 B.C., a famous tower was built in Pharos, now part of the city of Alexandria. It was 120 meters (393 feet) high and was one of the Seven Wonders of the World. Today, in addition to the traditional medium-range lighthouses, we also have radio beacons. They have a transmitter which automatically sends out signals at fixed intervals.

October 24

WHY DON'T SKYSCRAPERS FALL DOWN?

These tall buildings, which dominate the skyline in some big cities, are certainly not rigid in structure. If they were, they *would* fall down. On the contrary, they are designed and built in such a way that they

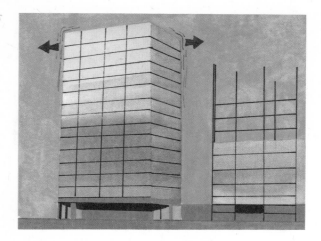

are quite flexible. In architectural terms, this is known as the co-efficient of elasticity . Skyscrapers sway slightly in strong winds and earth tremors. In fact, they are able to withstand quite strong earth tremors and quakes.

October 25

WHY DOES A BOOMERANG RETURN TO THE THROWER?

The returning boomerang is used by the natives of Australia, the Aborigines, mostly in sport. Its two arms are curved in opposite directions so it is similar to an airplane propeller. It is thrown with a special twisting

movement, and flies through the air and rotates at the same time. The speed of the boomerang keeps it rotating. Once the force from the throw has lessened, the boomerang stops its flight but still rotates. The force of its own weight and the turning movement enable it to return to the place where it started.

October 26

WHY IS POWDERED MILK MADE?

Essentially, powdered milk is fresh milk without any water, which normally makes up between 86 and 91 percent of its total content. When milk is dried, various interesting things happen: its weight is reduced by one tenth, its nutritious

properties remain unchanged and, if kept in air-tight containers, it lasts for several months.

October 27 — WHY ARE SHIPS LAUNCHED BACKWARDS?

If you have been at the launching of a new ship, or have seen it on television, you will have noticed that it goes down the launching slope backward. The back of the ship, called the stern, goes into the water first. There are several reasons for this. Firstly, it prevents the propellor being damaged. Secondly, because the lower part of the stern is smoother, contact with the water is easier. Finally, once the ship reaches the water, the wide shape of the upper part of the stern enables the hull to float more easily.

October 28 — WHY IS FOAM SOMETIMES USED TO PUT OUT FIRES?

Many fires, such as those in houses or buildings, or forests are put out with water. However, extinquishing foam was developed for fires involving liquids that burst into flames easily, such as gasoline, benzine, and alcohol. Because these liquids are lighter than water, the use of water could spread the fire rather than put it out. When foam spreads over a fire it acts as a kind of blanket and smothers the flames and puts the fire out. Small foam fire extinquishers are now available for use in the home or in cars and trucks.

October 29 — WHY IS A SPACESUIT SO BULKY?

Man can travel safely in space only if he is well protected against weightlessness, radiation, and extremes of pressure and temperature. Spacesuits are made up of several layers to give him this protection. That is why they are so bulky and clumsy, making movement difficult.

The spacesuits used by American astronauts are the result of many years research and cost a lot of money. One suit weighs 15 kgs (33 lbs) and consists of eight layers. The first layer is a chamber of air. The layers in contact with the astronaut's skin have a coil through which a cooling liquid flows to stabilize the body's temperature. The outside layer is aluminum and is designed to reflect the heat of the sun. Complete protection is given by the helmet, boots, and gloves.

 October 30 HOW DO CARS WITHOUT WHEELS MOVE?

 October 31 WHAT IS AN OIL TANKER?

Tankers are designed to carry liquid cargoes, usually crude oil, or petroleum. They are the biggest ships in use now. Most of them are too big to be able to use existing ports, and discharge their cargo by pipeline away from the shore at the end of long jetties. The inside of the tanker is divided into compartments for safety, to reduce the build up of gases, and prevent the ship capsizing from the movement of the liquid. The navigation bridge and crew's living quarters are in a superstructure at the stern.

At the present time, models such as Pegasus, designed in North America, and the cushioncraft, which is English, are just experimental. These prototypes offer the revolutionary innovation of having no wheels. They move by means of a cushion of air which keeps them half a meter (1½ feet) off the ground. In addition, they have a set of propellors enclosed in a tube at the back and the sides, that controls the level of propulsion which is limited to 65 kilometers (40 miles) per hour.

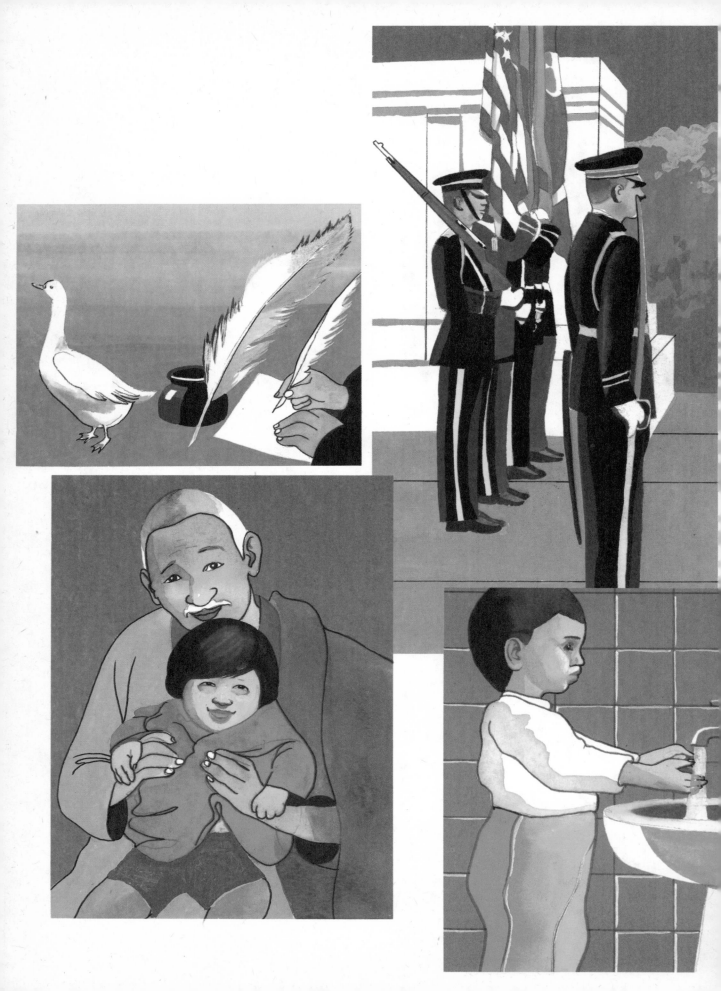

NOVEMBER

WHY SHOULD WE TREAT ELDERLY PEOPLE WITH RESPECT?

In most societies, past and present, elderly people have always been respected and given special treatment by those younger than themselves. They have experienced more than the young, and are respected for the wisdom they have gained.

Parents are often too busy or tired from work to talk to their children; while the grandparents have time to listen to their grandchildren and to tell them stories about life when they were young. How many of you find your grandparents fun to be with? Perhaps they like to give you treats and play games with you, and make you feel special.

The good thing is that old people are not only living longer, but stay stronger and healthier in old age, so your grandparents are likely to live longer than in days gone by.

November
2

WHY SHOULD WE CLEAN OUR TEETH?

When we eat, small pieces of food get trapped between our teeth. If they stay there the bacteria in our mouths will start to attack them, and this causes decay and infection which can destroy the teeth. Also, a substance called plaque builds up on the surface of our teeth near the gums, and this can be a breeding ground for bacteria. The more sugary food we eat, the more plaque builds up. So we need to brush our teeth with toothpaste regularly after meals.

November 3 — WHY SHOULD WE WASH OUR HANDS BEFORE EVERY MEAL?

In normal, everyday life, the germs on hands mixed with the perspiration that comes from skin, is a source of food for bacteria in the air. If we touch food with dirty hands, many of the germs would infect the food and could cause stomach upsets when we eat it. So we wash our hands before eating to get rid of the grease and germs on them.

November 4 — WHY SHOULD WE WASH OUR EARS?

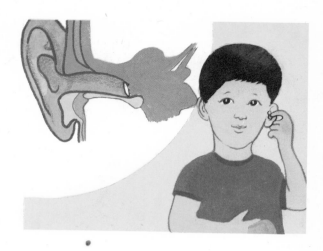

The inside of the ear is lined with a sticky, greasy substance called wax. This prevents dust and germs in the ear from going right inside the ear and causing infection. So we should wash our ears regularly to keep them clean and prevent wax from building up and causing deafness. Never poke anything into ears as you could easily cause damage to the eardrum.

November 5 — WHY IS IT BETTER TO EAT AT SET TIMES?

The process of digesting food takes a certain amount of time. It makes sense to eat at set times, leaving a sufficient amount of time between each meal for the stomach to digest the food. The stomach juices have

to break down the food so that it can be absorbed by the body.

Naturally, the times and sizes of meals vary from society to society, and habits and customs tend to decide these.

November 6 — WHY IS IT UNHEALTHY TO SMOKE?

The smoking habit came to Europe in the sixteenth century when tobacco was brought back from the United States. Smoking is a habit on which people easily become dependent, and it causes great damage to the human body. Tobacco contains a very toxic substance called nicotine, which is very bad for the respiratory (breathing) system, the heart, and the blood.

understand the world better, and hopefully improve it. Our education when we are children begins at home, then at school, by learning things that other people have discovered or done which are written in books, or skills they have developed. It is good to learn about many different things before choosing what we want to do as a career. After that, of course, it is up to us how much we continue to learn about different subjects.

November 8 — WHY DO COUNTRIES HAVE NATIONAL FLAGS?

November 7 — WHY SHOULD CHILDREN LEARN?

All through our lives we are always learning something new which helps us to

Groups of people who have the same religion, or are members of a special society, or are from the same country, usually have some sign or symbol which represents them. Christians have the symbol of the cross and Muslims have a half moon. The national flag, together with the national anthem, or song, is the symbol of a nation. Whenever people want to show that a representative of a nation or state is in a public building, ship, or embassy, the person's national flag is flown outside.

November 9

WHY DO WE HAVE TO PAY TAXES?

A tax is a sum of money which is paid by the citizens of a country to its government. Some taxes are direct, such as those you pay when you own certain things like a house or a car; others are added on to things you buy like electrical goods, and gasoline, or services such as repairs, building work, and restaurant meals. The government then claims the money back from the shops and service operators.

Taxes are the main income of the government and it uses this money to pay for public services such as roads, health, schools, police, and national defense. In democratic countries, people usually pay more or less tax according to how much they earn.

November 10

WHY DO PEOPLE IN SOME COUNTRIES HAVE IDENTITY CARDS?

In some countries, everybody over 18 years old has to carry an identity card which is proof of who they are. It contains important personal details such as their date of birth, their photograph, and fingerprints.

Apart from being a sure means of identification whenever necessary, an identity card makes it possible for authorities to keep a check on the citizens. In other countries, where there is more civil freedom, the identity card is not so important, and in some countries, such as Great Britain, it does not exist. British and American citizens have to use other forms of identification if they need them, such as a driver's license, credit card, or passport.

November 11 — WHY DO YOUNG MEN IN SOME COUNTRIES HAVE TO DO MILITARY SERVICE?

From the Middle Ages onward, most countries set up permanent armies to defend their homeland. In the eighteenth and nineteenth centuries, most armies adopted the system of compulsory military service, in which the leaders are professionals and the troops are recruited from the young men of the country. Nowadays there is a tendency for the length of military service to be fairly short (about a year or so), and for it to include

extra education. Sometimes the recruits carry out tasks of national interest or public service. But if their country went to war they would be called on to fight.

November 12 — WHY DO WE HAVE TO GO TO SCHOOL?

Although we start to learn as soon as we are born, it is at school that this learning becomes more ordered. School, as well as teaching us necessary knowledge for everyday life, also helps us to develop our personalities, and educates us to live together and realize that everyone else is as important as we are.

November 13 — WHAT IS THE HIGHWAY CODE FOR?

Once factories started to build large numbers of cars more people began to use them, and as a result more accidents happened. So a set of rules was formed which everyone using the road must obey. This is called the highway code, and it helps to make the traffic move in a controlled way and improves safety for drivers and pedestrians. Drivers have to know the highway code to pass their driving

test, and should continue to keep up-to-date with new rules and road signs.

Traffic police make sure that people follow the rules of the highway code. Even so, the number of road accidents is still enormous, usually because drivers are not careful enough.

November 14

WHY DO AMBULANCES AND FIRE ENGINES HAVE SIRENS?

When it is a question of saving someone's life, the most important thing is speed. Two of the clearest examples of this are when someone is very ill or has had an accident, and when there is a disaster such as a house on fire.

In the first case, the patient has to be taken to the hospital as quickly as possible; in the second, help must get to the place where people are in danger as quickly as possible. So ambulances and fire engines have sirens which they use when driving at

high speed or through heavy traffic, to warn other drivers to get out of the way, and let them drive as fast as they can.

November 15

WHY DO SOME PUBLIC PLACES HAVE STATUES?

Throughout history there have been men and women who have been highly thought of by their governments or fellow citizens. To honor and remember such people it became the custom to build statues of them in public places.

There are also statues built which commemorate a whole group of people, or an important event. A well-made statue adds elegance and beauty to the place where it stands.

November 16

WHY DO WE HAVE MOTHER'S DAY?

Most of us feel very grateful and loving towards our mothers as it is they who love and look after us from the day we are born. A great deal of importance is attached to mothers in our society, and always has been. This is why there is a special day each year, known as Mother's Day, when we show our gratitude by giving flowers or small presents.

November 17

WHY DO WE KISS EACH OTHER?

A kiss is the traditional sign of affection. We kiss each other, especially on the lips, which are a very sensitive part of the body, to show fondness for each other. We also use kisses in a more formal way, usually on the cheek, or even on the hand, as a friendly or polite form of greeting.

November 18

WHY DO WE SHAKE HANDS WITH OUR RIGHT HANDS?

The Western custom of shaking hands has its origins in the past. Centuries ago men carried weapons, usually in their right hands (most people are right-handed). When one man wanted to show friendship to another, he threw down his weapons and offered his empty right hand to the other person as a sign of peace. The custom has remained.

You should shake hands firmly as it is a sign of friendliness or agreement, and a limp, weak handshake does not seem genuine. But you have to be careful not to overdo it, and hurt the other person's hand!

November 19

WHY ARE CITIES BUILT?

Although the first cities appeared many centuries ago, as centers of culture and civilization and commerce, the city in its modern sense is largely a result of the Industrial Revolution of the eighteenth century. At this time, large numbers of houses were built near the factories that were constructed as industry developed. Huge numbers of people came from the countryside to work in the cities.

Today cities still attract people wanting work, and many have become very large and overcrowded areas.

information or send messages. This need gave birth to writing, which is a visible form of the languages we speak. Sometimes words were carved into stone or clay, sometimes written with ink on paper. There are many different ways of writing, as, like speech, it developed independently throughout the world – Chinese letters represent ideas and objects, while European and Asian languages are based on the sounds of words.

November
21

WHY ARE SKYSCRAPERS SO TALL?

The great number of people living in cities has made lack of space a big problem. By building skyscrapers, builders have tried to make the most of what space

November
20

WHY WAS WRITING INVENTED?

Man's first systems of communication were, of course, signs and speech. But a system was needed which could record, keep, and pass on knowledge and

there is, so that cities have grown upward rather than outward. As land is private property in Western societies, it is obviously more profitable for owners to build structures with many floors, each of which can then be sold or rented. New York, one of the most densely populated cities in the world, is famous for the variety and number of its skyscrapers.

November 22

WHY DO WE HAVE UNDERGROUND RAILWAYS?

Underground railways, known as the underground or tube in Britain, the subway in America, the metro in France and Spain and the U-Bahn in Germany, answer the need for fast, efficient public transport in large cities. This underground transport has all sorts of advantages: it does not interfere with the various forms of traffic on the surface; it runs on electricity so it does not pollute the air, and rarely has accidents. There are underground railways in many of the big cities of the world.

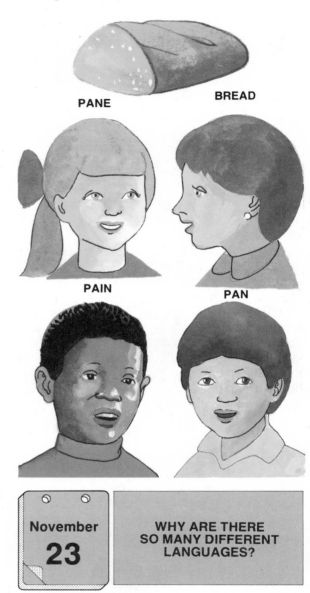

PANE

BREAD

PAIN

PAN

November 23

WHY ARE THERE SO MANY DIFFERENT LANGUAGES?

Although there seem to be a lot of totally different languages, many are very similar to each other. Long ago when people lived in groups and communities without being able to travel very much, they did develop their own languages. But as transportation improved, enabling people to travel more, and as small countries were conquered by larger empires, languages became more mixed. The Roman Empire, which conquered many parts of Europe, took their language, Latin, to all those countries. French, Italian, Spanish and Rumanian all come from Latin, and there are many Latin words in the English language. English, Dutch, German and Scandinavian belong to the Indo-European family of languages.

November 24

WHY IS PLAYING IMPORTANT?

Some adults think that when children play they are wasting their time and that it is more important to study. They couldn't be more wrong. Children need to play both by themselves and with others because they develop their personalities this way. Babies especially learn through playing, and children's games change as they grow up, until they reach an age where they are gradually replaced by other activities and pastimes. Adults do not play in the same way as children, but they also need leisure interests – more than ever now that working hours are less – both to amuse themselves and to relax.

November 25

WHY DO SOME PEOPLE DRINK AN APERITIF BEFORE DINNER?

The custom of eating or drinking something before dinner is known as having an aperitif. This word comes from Latin, and means an "opener" or something that whets the appetite. In ancient times its purpose was to stimulate the stomach juices ready for food, but today it is more of a social custom.

November 26

WHERE DOES THE WORD PEN COME FROM?

The Latin word for feather is "penna" and since ancient times people have used bird feathers, especially goose feathers, for

writing and drawing. The bottom end was sharpened and dipped in ink, which filled the hollow stem of the feather. These were known as quill pens and they were commonly used until the end of the last century. The word pen now means any implement for writing or drawing which consists of a nib of some kind attached to a holder for the ink.

November 27

WHY DO SOME PEOPLE USE SIGN LANGUAGE?

Deaf and dumb people are often born deaf. Because they cannot hear sounds they are unable to copy them, so they do not learn to talk. They are able to see, though, and use sign language, a system of

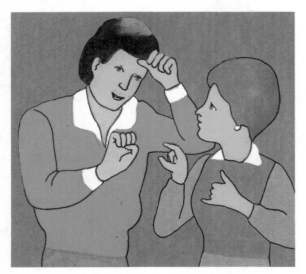

hand gestures which correspond to letters and words of the alphabet.

More recently, new methods of teaching have been introduced; the person learns to talk by copying the lip movements and vibrations in the throat of the teacher. They can understand what other people say by carefully watching their mouths and lips (lip reading).

November 28

WHY DO DOORS HAVE KEYHOLES?

People have always used locks on doors to keep houses safe from enemies and wild animals. Old systems, such as a bar or bolt across the door, had a big disadvantage; they could only be locked from the inside, when somebody was indoors.

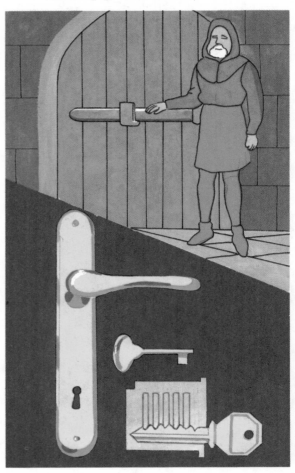

When mechanical locks and keyholes were invented, this problem was solved, as the door could be locked from either inside or outside, and each household could have a different lock and key. Keyholes today are much smaller and very secure, though extra bolts are often used on the inside.

only those with poor sight are allowed to use one. It is partly for feeling the way, and partly so that people will recognize that the owner is blind, and will help him.

HOW DO BLIND PEOPLE READ?

Although blind people cannot see, their sense of touch becomes far more developed than that of most sighted people. This ability was put to use by a brilliant blind man called Louis Braille, who in the early nineteenth century invented a system of writing which bears his name. The Braille system reproduces the letters of the alphabet by a series of dots in certain positions, which are raised on the paper. The blind person runs the tips of his fingers across the pages of the Braille book, and can work out the printed letters and numbers. In this way, he "reads" the book, using his sense of touch in the same way as a sighted person uses sight.

WHY DO SOME PEOPLE USE A WHITE STICK?

Not long ago, every gentleman carried a walking stick, and around the turn of the century no "elegant" man would be seen without one. There was even a different stick for each part of the day. Nowadays, they are not generally used except by blind people and those who cannot walk very well. A blind person's stick is white, and

ORIGINAL FRENCH BRAILLE

LETTER W WAS ADDED

DECEMBER

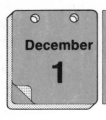

WHY ARE FINGERPRINTS NEEDED ON SOME IDENTITY PAPERS?

The curved lines in the skin on the tips of fingers make a different pattern in every single person, and do not change. This was known centuries ago by Mesapotamian and Chinese people and recognized by the Italian anatomist Marcello Malpighi in the seventeenth century.

When fingers are pressed onto ink and then onto paper they leave an impression of the curved lines behind, and these were named fingerprints by the English scientist Francis Galton. The system has been perfected as a way of tracing and identifying criminals. Fingerprints are now included in personal identity papers in some countries as an extra precaution and a way of identifying people.

MARCELLO MALPIGHI

WHY DO WE VOTE?

In a democratic society we need to elect a few people who are best suited to representing everyone else and their interests when making the laws for their country. Depending on the number of people involved, there are two types of vote: direct and indirect. When it is direct voting, everyone chooses freely between candidates; in indirect voting, a restricted number of suitable people are selected, and others then vote and choose between them. The age of majority, which is when you become legally able to vote, varies from country to country, but in many countries it is eighteen years of age.

WHY DO WE NEED PASSPORTS?

No country likes to admit criminals, or people who might, for political reasons, be dangerous to its government, such as spies. So everyone entering a foreign country needs a passport to identify who he is. The passport is a small booklet which contains a description of its owner's

Although in Europe knives date from Paleolithic times, and spoons from the Bronze Age, they were not used at the table, and nor was the fork until the eighteenth century. Since meat was the main food it was cut up first into pieces and then eaten with the hands. Now, everybody in the West eats with cutlery; it would be considered bad manners not to. It prevents germs on the hands touching food, and grease covering our hands.

However, some Eastern countries have different traditions. In India and South Asia, for instance, the fingertips of the right hand are used for eating. The Chinese and Japanese people use two sticks called chopsticks to eat everything, even soup!

appearance, plus a photograph. There are empty pages for officials at seaports and airports to stamp the date of entry or exit from a country. Unless children have to travel alone, which is unusual, they are included on their parent's passport.

December 4

WHY DO WE USE CUTLERY?

December 5

WHY IS NUMBER 13 THOUGHT TO BE UNLUCKY?

Of all the traditional superstitions the one about number 13 is probably the most widespread. In the Bible, there were thirteen people at the Last Supper – Jesus and his twelve disciples – and it was the thirteenth person, Judas, who betrayed Jesus. This is why 13 is an unlucky number. The feeling is so deeply rooted that this number is often left out of a series of numbers in daily life, such as house numbers.

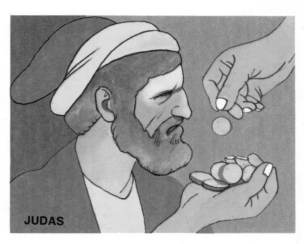

JUDAS

December 6

WHY DO WE PUT OUR HANDS IN FRONT OF OUR MOUTHS WHEN WE YAWN?

Yawning is a reflex action and we do it for many reasons. It is caused by hunger, tiredness, or boredom. When we yawn, the mouth and the glottis in our throat open together, and we breathe out gastric smells which are unpleasant for those near to us. For this reason, it is polite to put our hands in front of our mouths. Yawning also has the peculiar characteristic of being "catching," and if we don't cover our mouths, everyone near to us will start to yawn too!

December 7

WHY DO PEOPLE DANCE?

Dancing is one of the oldest human activities. It probably started with ritual

ceremonies. When men went off on hunting trips they would dance to imitate a successful hunt. Sometimes they danced to persuade the gods to send rain, or protect them from disease. The Navaho Indians in the U.S.A. have a famous rain dance. These rituals developed into dancing for pleasure. Country dancing was fun for everyone during holidays, and most countries now have their own national dances. Dancing is still a favorite activity for all age groups.

December 8

WHY DO TROUSER LEGS HAVE CREASES?

The habit of putting creases in trousers was not originally a question of taste or of looks, but of sheer chance. After America had been discovered, clothes had to be shipped from Europe to people in the colonies. The trousers were just piled up in the hold during the long crossing, and they ended up with a crease pressed into them which people did not bother to get rid of. The crease became a custom, and now men's trousers seem odd without them!

December
9

WHY DO CARICATURES MAKE US LAUGH?

Although the name caricature is a modern one, the art itself has very old roots. Even fifth century pottery has these figures on it, and the way they make us smile has hardly changed. Caricatures are pictures which deliberately exaggerate someone's features and make them look funny or ridiculous; sometimes they can be

very cruel. Caricatures of politicians in the newspapers are called cartoons.

December
10

WHY DO SOME COUNTRIES HAVE A CARNIVAL IN SPRING?

This custom started in Roman times with the celebrations and worship of the god Saturn. It then took on more of a Christian meaning when it became a break from normal routine just before Lent. Until the nineteenth century, it was one of the most lively festivals of several countries.

Today, although the carnival has partly kept its original features – disguises, masks, the crowning of a mock king – it has lost its primitive meaning. The carnival in Rio de Janeiro is a festival famous all over the world. Carnival time is a happy event when everyone can enjoy themselves.

169

December 11 — WHY DO SOME MONUMENTS HAVE AN ETERNAL FLAME?

A light which is constantly burning has always had a deep significance. For instance, beneath the Arc de Triomphe in Paris and on the tomb in Arlington of a former President of the U.S.A., John F. Kennedy, there are eternal flames, or constantly burning torches. They are there to commemorate those who gave their lives for their country.

December 12 — HOW DO MUSICAL INSTRUMENTS PRODUCE SOUND?

SOUND WAVES

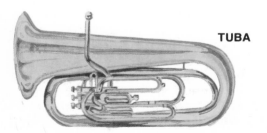

TUBA

Most instruments are hollow, but not closed, so the air can come and go freely. You may have noticed that if you tap a hollow box it makes a more lasting sound than if you tap a solid block of wood. Perhaps you've tried blowing across the top of an empty bottle, or listened to the wind making a whistling sound through the trees. These are musical sounds. The same thing happens when musicians play real instruments; they make the air inside vibrate. The vibrations set up sound waves, and this is what you hear.

December 13 — WHY DO WE ENJOY LISTENING TO MUSIC?

Music, dance, drama, art and literature are called the arts. They are all things we can enjoy. Music can make us happy or sad, lively or quiet. In a Western society, listening to music, whether it's live – at a loud pop concert or to a classical symphony orchestra – or on records or radio, is considered a relaxing and enjoyable pastime.

In contrast, loud noises from machinery or traffic can be very irritating.

December 14 — WHY DO WE HAVE NATIONAL ANTHEMS?

Most countries have a national anthem. They are songs written at some time in a nation's history to glorify a nation's ideals or achievements. God Save the King/Queen was adopted as the British national anthem to unify everyone in support of the monarch when people were rioting in the 1820s. The French Marseillaise glorified the ideals of the French Revolution. Nowadays we sing these anthems at public parades and some public performances of music or theater.

December 15 — WHY DO CARS DRIVE ON THE LEFT IN BRITAIN?

In Britain and certain other countries cars drive on the left. It is said that this goes back to the days of the coach and horses.

The coachman used his right hand to whip the horses, and this would have meant great danger to people walking along the side of the road if he had driven the coach on the righthand side of the road. So he drove it on the left. In Britain and countries that are part of the British Commonwealth, the custom has remained to this day.

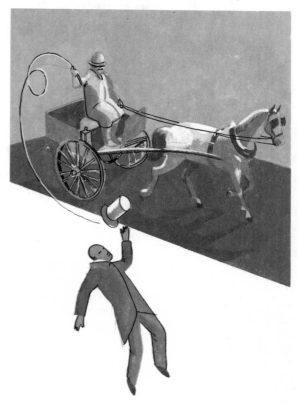

December 16 — WHY DO SOME PEOPLE LIVE IN CARAVANS?

The nomadic, or traveling, way of life has always been characteristic of some communities and tribes. In ancient times, sometimes entire communities would migrate, and even now many primitive tribes or peoples, especially African or Aboriginal, regularly move on as the seasons change. They go to different places where they can find food, or simply because it is their custom to do so.

European gypsy families, whose origins go back to the ninth century, still live in

times and tied. The tie we know, with its knot and the ends hanging down the front of the shirt, did not come into common use until this century. It has no practical purpose but is usually part of any uniform, and is worn on formal occasions and by businessmen.

caravans, moving on from time to time. Caravans kept on permanent camp sites have become the only way for some people to own their own home.

December
17

WHY DO PEOPLE WEAR TIES?

The tie comes directly from the lace neck tie which was worn by men in the seventeenth century. During the French Revolution it changed to a simple piece of material wrapped around the neck several

December
18

WHY IS JUSTICE ALWAYS REPRESENTED BY A PAIR OF SCALES?

The aim of justice is to give each person whatever belongs to him by right, and to defend people in a fair way. Justice is one of the most important virtues, and when represented as a statue is shown as a blindfolded noble lady carrying a sword (the law) and a pair of scales (fairness). The blindfold shows that justice is impartial, and does not take sides.

December
19

WHAT IS THE DECLARATION OF HUMAN RIGHTS?

The gradual move of civilized societies towards more perfect justice led the French humanists to draw up a Declaration of Human Rights in 1789. Recently, representatives from countries all over the world met in the city of Helsinki to discuss and bring these guidelines up to date. They signed a document to say their governments would act according to the different points which are contained in the Declaration, including freedom of expression and freedom of movement and development.

December
20

WHAT IS THE UNITED NATIONS ORGANIZATION

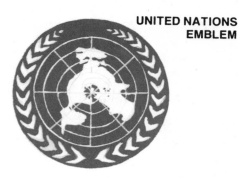

UNITED NATIONS EMBLEM

This organization, sometimes called the UNO, has its headquarters in New York. After the Second World War many people felt that a place where all nations could send their representatives to discuss the problems and wars of the world could help to prevent a Third World War. Many countries became members at that time.

The UN maintains a peace-keeping force, soldiers of many different nationalities, who are sent to countries where peace is threatened. It also runs many aid organizations. The Security Council for example watches over freedom and security in the world. UNESCO looks after education, science and culture. UNICEF is concerned with the welfare of children.

December
21

WHY DO WE GIVE TIPS?

We give a tip, or a present of money, to someone who has given us particularly

173

good service, to show our appreciation of the care they have taken, in a restaurant or at the hairdresser's for example. Strictly speaking, it is money to buy a drink for themselves, and in other languages this meaning is clear: "tip" in German is "das Trinkgeld," and in French "la pourboire." In the past people who received these tips were often badly paid by their employers. Now there are laws to make employers pay better wages, tips are not so important.

December
22

WHY DO WE LAUGH WHEN PEOPLE TRIP?

When we see someone such as a clown fall over, we laugh, but more at the funny side of the act of falling over than at the person, especially when we know that

he is not hurt. When people fall and hurt themselves, we don't laugh.

On the other hand, by making themselves ridiculous and falling over on purpose, clowns deliberately make us feel secure and superior, and so we laugh at them because they are so foolish. Great comedians such as Charlie Chaplin made use of these situations and that was why they were so popular.

December
23

WHY IS HYGIENE SO IMPORTANT?

Although it is true that people knew, even in Greek and Roman times, that cleanliness and hygiene were important, it wasn't until the great discoveries about bacteria in the nineteenth century that we knew why. Until then, plagues and epidemics destroyed whole populations, and the average lifespan was much shorter than it is today.

Hygiene includes many aspects: personal hygiene and hygiene at work. Health laws exist to enforce hygiene in all aspects of public life, and the standards are regulated by the International Convention of the World Health Organization. However, poor countries without proper sewage systems and clean drinking water still suffer from diseases like typhus which are carried in water.

December 24

WHAT IS A SWORN STATEMENT?

A patent is a copyright for a new invention, which describes it in very great detail to stop other people from stealing the idea. When a foreign patent has to be translated into English to be used as the patent, it is important that the translation is accurate. The translator has to swear that it is a faithful translation and sign it in front of someone who is legally qualified to witness oaths. So the translation is a sworn document.

December 25

WHY DO PEOPLE PAINT PICTURES?

When we paint pictures, we usually want to say something about the world around us. At school we may be asked to paint pictures of our family or home, or pictures about the things we are learning there. It is all part of learning to look at the world and understand it.

Artists who paint for a living are doing the same thing. Sometimes they paint portraits of famous people. They may paint pictures to illustrate books, or for advertisements in magazines. However, many artists also want to paint pictures which tell us what they feel about the world.

December 26

WHY IS ATHLETICS GOOD FOR YOU?

Athletics is a form of physical education which carefully develops and exercises the different parts of the human body, and improves the athlete's overall health, both in mind and in body. Athletics was practiced in ancient civilizations, and classical Greece made athletics famous with their well-known Olympic Games and their high standards. Today, athletics is a discipline which has been scientifically developed, is recommended by doctors, and is practiced all over the world at local, national, and international meetings.

December 27

WHY DO WE NEED TO HELP THE THIRD WORLD COUNTRIES?

Although it may seem hard to believe in our prosperous societies, only 28 per cent of the world's population is well-fed. In many African countries and other poor areas people do not have enough food. This means that half of the world's children under five are undernourished or hungry, and this harms both their physical and their intellectual development. We need to support schemes to help people in these countries as much as possible, in as many ways as possible. Sometimes this is by sending food or money, especially at times of special need such as drought and crop failure. In the long term we need to help them build wells for clean water, teach them basic hygiene, and how to make the best use of their resources.

December 28

WHY ARE SOME PEOPLE MEMBERS OF THE NOBILITY?

The idea of a sovereign's giving noble titles to people goes back centuries. The aim was to distinguish in some way those citizens who gave great service to their king and country. In Germany and Spain, especially, titles were given for great military deeds. At the beginning of the Middle Ages nobles in Europe had great political power, but this power weakened. Now, when a reigning sovereign gives people these titles it is almost always in recognition of great talent in a particular field, such as science or the arts, or for public service.

December 29

WHY DO BANKNOTES HAVE A WATERMARK?

Frequent forgery of legal banknotes has forced experts to come up with this way of making the forgery of banknotes more difficult. A watermark is made in the paper itself when it is manufactured, and it is very difficult to copy this.

from over 100 nations take part. There are about 20 sports, of which the most important are track and field athletics.

The idea for these competitive events came from Ancient Greece. And the spirit of the games has always been one of true sportsmanship; that is, fair competition, without the aid of cheating in any form. However, competition is so fierce these days that it is hard for competitors to live up to these ideals.

December 31 — WHY DO GAMES REFEREES USE WHISTLES?

This custom started by accident. In New Zealand in 1833, a Mr. Attack, the referee of a football match, couldn't make himself heard above the noise of the over-excited players, so had the bright idea of resorting to a whistle. The response was immediate — the players were so surprised that they stopped playing right away. This was so effective that whistles have been used by referees ever since.

December 30 — WHAT ARE THE OLYMPIC GAMES?

The Olympic Games is the biggest sporting event in the world. It takes place every four years, each time in a different country. Amateur sportsmen and women

JANUARY

FEBRUARY

MARCH

APRIL

MAY

JUNE

JULY

AUGUST

SEPTEMBER

OCTOBER

NOVEMBER

DECEMBER